THE CITY OF TH

# THE CITY OF THE HEART

## YUNUS EMRE'S VERSES OF WISDOM AND LOVE

TRANSLATION BY
SÜHA FAIZ

Preface by
John D. Norton
*Director, Centre for Turkish Studies, Durham*

# ELEMENT

Shaftesbury, Dorset ● Rockport, Massachusetts

© Süha Faiz 1992

Published in Great Britain in 1992 by
Element Books Limited
Longmead, Shaftesbury, Dorset

Published in the USA in 1992 by
Element, Inc
42 Broadway, Rockport, MA 01966

Cover from an illustration by the Translator
(Stylised script recording
a saying of the Prophet Mohammed:
'Who knows himself knows his Lord')
Cover design by Barbara McGavin
Designed by Roger Lightfoot
Typeset by Footnote Graphics, Warminster
Printed and bound in Great Britain by
Billings Ltd, Hylton Road, Worcester

British Library Cataloguing in Publication Data

Emre, Yunus
The city of the heart: Yunus Emre's verses of
wisdom and love.
I. Title
894.3513

ISBN 1-85230-333-6

SOS re Computer —
could you possibly come
in for a moment? It's
not behaving.

Lalage Fair

Dear Mr + Mrs Fair,

EVENTS AT THE MEDIEVAL HALL – 24 May to 28 M

This coming week is rather busier than usual and so I thou
our plans.

Tuesday 24$^{th}$ (6pm to approx 8pm) – A drinks reception

Wednesday 25$^{th}$ (6pm to 11pm) – A social gathering whic
minutes towards the start of the evening (inside The Hall)
until 1015pm.

Friday 27$^{th}$ – A civil wedding ceremony at 1pm followe
music).

Saturday 28$^{th}$ – A civil wedding ceremony at 1130am fol
civil wedding ceremony at 3.30pm followed by a short dr
the evening from 8pm until 10.30pm consisting of a meal

This book
is dedicated
to
ERHAN ŞAHİNGÜR
who gave me the verses
and to
MY FAMILY
who moved me to translate them

For David Postle — friend for more than 10 years —
in token of deep regard,

Süha Fâin

14 June 2005

(See pages 196–197
of Chapter 9 of my "memoires")

# CONTENTS

Preface    ix

Origins    xii

Translator's Foreword    xv

Introduction    1

YUNUS EMRE'S VERSES OF WISDOM AND LOVE    5

Notes    122

Glossary    125

Index of Turkish initial lines    131

# PREFACE

Yunus Emre offered to the whole world a timeless message of tolerance and humanity. He did so in Turkish of imperishable appeal, and Turkish speakers find his verses as irresistible today as they did six centuries ago. They turn to them for inspiration, for consolation, for insight into eternal truths, and for sheer delight in the language.

His message is universal, but until now those who do not know Turkish have had scant opportunity to hear it. Acquaintance with that message is one of the greatest privileges enjoyed by foreigners who have learned Turkish. They readily appreciate the reward they have gained, but their natural desire to share this treasure with a wider audience has been frustrated by the language barrier. Sometimes such partial translations as they have encountered or attempted have merely served to heighten that frustration. Consequently, other people have only been able to glimpse a few of the beauties of Yunus Emre, and then through a glass darkly. Tantalizingly, they could sense that here was something of inestimable value, yet most of it was beyond the grasp their translations allowed.

This situation, though regrettable, was understandable. It is an awesome challenge for any translator to convey the profound philosophies of Yunus Emre in similar sublime, yet seemingly simple, verse. Past attempts were often doomed to founder, either on the rocks of pedantry or on the shoals of shallow poetry.

Now, in this translation by Süha Faiz, we have a mirror that lets the English reader see the meaning of Yunus Emre's verses expressed with a fluency and verve that in their impact reflect the appeal and excitement of the original. In his foreword Süha Faiz modestly says that he has striven to remain faithful to the spirit of Yunus Emre without slavishly maintaining the rhyme. In my opinion he has indeed been true to the spirit of the original. But he has done more. In opening a window to the wisdom of the Orient, he has also produced a work of literature which will give enduring pleasure to readers of English. The result is a work that is deeply satisfying on many different planes.

Through his verses Yunus Emre speaks of the all-consuming spirit of love – love of God, love of one's fellow man, love of nature. A love that sees something of God in everyone, a love that underlies the Sufi concept dear to so many mystics: the unity of existence. A love that speaks straight to the heart of man, revealing exalted mysteries to the humble and receptive, and uniting man with God. That love shines through this translation, every line of which reveals itself to be a labour of love as well as one of very great skill.

Yunus Emre's life is known to us through legends rather than reliable records, and the facts of his life continue to be a subject of academic dispute. It is generally accepted that he lived in Anatolia from about the middle of the thirteenth century until around the end of the first quarter of the fourteenth century. Some argue that he was illiterate, others that he completed an advanced theological education. Still today there are several dervish orders claiming him as one of their members. The details are inconclusive, and that seems appropriate, for Yunus Emre's message of love and humanity is boundless and not to be diminished by trying to fit it within the confines of any single dogma. This great poet's proper destiny is to remain for ever above the different rules, regulations and restrictions imposed on the followers of any one mystic path.

We do know a great deal about conditions in Anatolia when Yunus was alive. They were troubled times. Religious, political, ethnic and social differences divided man from fellow man, but Yunus Emre looked beyond these differences, pointing to what men have in common. As will be apparent to readers of these verses, he also looked beyond his own times and his own compatriots. Through this translation that spans centuries and continents as well as languages, he speaks to us today in our dangerous, divided, and fast-changing world.

It is therefore particularly fitting that UNESCO should have chosen to make 1991 'International Yunus Emre Year'. And it is an especially happy coincidence that this English version by Süha Faiz should make its appearance in time for 1991.

I am intrigued to discover from the translator's foreword that his introduction to Yunus Emre was the same as my own: through the verses given in a certain Turkish Reader. Fortunately, my next acquaintance was not as long delayed as his. As my subsequent career has been centred round Turkish Studies, I have been able to see for myself over many years how Turks of all generations have

remained under Yunus Emre's spell. The innumerable editions of
his collected works, complete with commentaries and studies of his
life, as well as the extracts that adorn countless anthologies and
school textbooks, testify to his enduring appeal. At many different
Sufi gatherings I have heard his verses used in prayers, sung in
hymns, and quoted in instruction; and I have often heard the same
verses quoted with equal enthusiasm by secularist disciples of
Kemal Atatürk.

Yunus Emre's message is indeed one which transcends sectarian
boundaries. His words appeal to the human heart and get to the
heart of the human condition. They also lodge in the memory and
come frequently to mind, bidden or unbidden; they never fail to
please. Everyone is the better for knowing Yunus Emre. Now an
English-speaking audience can share this rich heritage and can
delight in the language of this translation.

I have the greatest pleasure in commending it.

John D. Norton
Director, Centre for Turkish Studies,
Durham.

# ORIGINS

Something I owe to the soil that grew –
More to the life that fed –
But most to Allah who gave me two
Separate sides to my head.
(from Rudyard Kipling's *Kim*)

Like Kim (which, curiously, happens to mean 'who?' in Turkish),
Fate has made me a man of two worlds. I am a Turk from the island
of Cyprus. When I was born at Famagusta in 1926, Cyprus had
been a British Crown Colony for a little under a year, although
Britain had in fact began to administer the island, as part of the
Ottoman Empire, in 1878. My father, believing that an English
education would best fit his children for the world which seemed to
be coming, saw that from their earliest years they were brought up
in English schools. This education began when I was five at a
boarding-school in Kyrenia, opened by three adventurous young
English girls and run on Froebel principles. By the time I eventu-
ally finished school in England, and left university there at the age
of twenty, I had been separated from my parents and from Cyprus
for twelve years. My father died during the war when I was fourteen.

At twenty-three I was in the old Colonial Service – first in the
Gold Coast (Ghana), and then back in Cyprus, before and during
Archbishop Makarios's EOKA campaign for *enosis* ('union': of
Cyprus with Greece). In 1960, when the Republic of Cyprus was
set up, intended to be the means (so soon to be aborted) by which
the Greek and Turkish peoples of the island could live together, I
left Cyprus with my English wife and two children to live in
England; and we have done so ever since.

The first Turkish Reader I had used when keeping up my Turkish
in Africa had contained four quatrains by Yunus Emre, and these
are included in Verse 123 of this book. The sentiments must have
touched a deep chord in me for the words have always stayed with
me. I read nothing more by, or about, Yunus Emre until 1976.

That year my wife and I went to Turkey for a fortnight's holiday. Towards the end of our stay at a small hotel in Alanya, I heard a Turkish father call out to his young son who was splashing about in the swimming pool: he addressed the child by name – 'Emre'. I asked if he had named the boy after Yunus Emre and, on the spur of the moment, quoted the last of the quatrains I still remembered – the final one of Verse 123. To his enquiry I said that I had for more than twenty-five years been greatly interested in Turkey and its language, and had acquired fluency while in Cyprus. I mentioned that we were to fly back to London a couple of days later via Istanbul, from Antalya, about a hundred miles along the coast. I learned that he was a bank official in Antalya taking a weekend break with his family in Alanya. He left later that day.

We were due to take off from Antalya early in the morning and had cut things pretty fine for catching our connecting flight to Istanbul. As we rushed out of the taxi and into the airport building with only a few minutes to spare, there stood Emre's father holding a paper parcel. I was taken aback at seeing him there, especially at such an hour, and in the last-minute turmoil of getting on the aeroplane I barely had time to thank him for coming to see us off and for the present which he thrust into my hand. On the aeroplane I unwrapped what I had thought might be a box of Turkish Delight or something similar. It was in fact a handsomely bound gilt-blocked book entitled *Yunus Emre ve Tasavvuf* (*Yunus Emre and Mysticism*).

As I read these verses over the next few years, I began to wonder if I might one day try to put them into English, if only to enable my wife and children to have some idea of the original. On my retirement some years later I settled down to the task and as a daily routine over the years I managed to complete what I had started – the product of a gift to me by a generous spirit following a casual meeting.

This translation is, therefore, in the nature of a personal testimony to that spirit and to the reality I see in Yunus's verses. It may well also have been that I was moved to undertake such a daunting work in the unconscious hope that those whose knowledge of things Turkish and Islamic is possibly still derived from a limited view imposed by historical circumstances, might through Yunus Emre be given a new vista and fresh insight. Certainly as I have searched in my heart and head for the words with which to interpret the Turkish text, I have felt an increasing bond with the man who recorded his own feelings so long ago. I hope that something of his spirit may shine through the double veil of words through which any translation must pass. I hope too that these translations may be received in that spirit voiced in Shakespeare's *Sonnet XXXII*:

> If thou survive my well-contented day,
> When that churl Death my bones with dust will cover,
> And shalt by fortune once more re-survey
> These poor rude lines of thy deceased lover,
> Compare them with the bettering of the time,
> And though they be outstripped by every pen,
> *Reserve them for my love, not for their rhyme,*
> Exceeded by the height of happier men.
> Oh then vouchsafe me but this loving thought:
> 'Had my friend's Muse grown with this growing age,
> A dearer birth than this his love had brought,
> To march in ranks of better equipage:
>   But since he died, and poets better prove,
>   *Theirs for their style I'll read, his for his love'.*

(Translator's italics.)

# TRANSLATOR'S FOREWORD

My endeavour in making this translation has been to produce an English text which departs as little as possible from the sense, spirit, and structure of the original Turkish; to achieve the practically impossible aim of enabling English readers to feel that they are hearing the original author speaking to them across the years. But anyone who attempts to translate poetry must of necessity sacrifice something of the original. It is virtually impossible always to reproduce the images in the same syntax, and with the identical harmony and rhyme, when moving from one language to another, especially when those languages are as different as are Turkish and English.

The basic unit of Yunus's poetry is the couplet, though nearly all these could from the interior rhymes also be conceived as quatrains. For the greater part I have conformed to Yunus's metrical rhythm, or beat. I have also aimed to contain his images within that structure in language which conveys his spirit as faithfully as I have been able, but which sacrifices his rhyme. This latter, peculiarly suited in the original to the vowel-harmonic quality of Turkish, can if blindly and slavishly reproduced come perilously close to doggerel. As an illustration I give the following verses of my own to show the form, rhyme, and metrical shape that Yunus commonly adopts:

> Yunus Emre not by art, by feeling reaches human heart,
> Rends the veil which keeps apart, teaches magnanimity.

> Yunus who in earthly life found that peace might come of strife,
> That even bloody sword and knife may lead man to humanity.

> Yunus Emre, man of God, shows the path for those who plod
> In faith the steps he too has trod – the Path to true tranquillity.

As to the Turkish in which Yunus Emre wrote, this is easier for a present-day Turk to understand than Chaucer in the original is for a modern-English speaker, even though Chaucer lived about a generation later than Yunus. Just as Chaucer wrote in the evolving 'English tongue' which 'all understanden' (a blend of Anglo-Saxon and Norman French), so Yunus too wrote in popular Turkish accessible to everyone. Over the next six and a half centuries of the Ottoman Empire, the language both of the Court and of the educated Ottoman citizen (*Osmanlı*) acquired such a heavy accretion of Persian and Arabic vocabulary and grammatical focus that it became incomprehensible to the ordinary person. Thus Kemal Atatürk, the founder of modern Turkey, made the reformation of the language one of his first tasks, not only by changing from the Arabic to a Latin script but by encouraging the movement to replace foreign words by indigenous ones drawn from the historic Turkish tongue. As a result, the language of Yunus is near enough to today's Turkish to be understood (at a certain depth) by any modern Turkish speaker, though not without some difficulty at times.

Nonetheless Yunus was a Moslem mystic and he inevitably used terms in Arabic, the language of the Koran, the Revealed Book of Islam. Even so, he often took purely Turkish terms for such concepts as Unity and Love, and sometimes ascribed to God not the Arabic *Allah* but the pre-Islamic Turkish words for the Divinity, *Tanrı* and *Chalap*.

It is appropriate to explain here the method of spelling and transliteration I have used. The Turkish text from which I worked was published in Turkey in 1961, and accordingly it appears in the modern Turkish Latin script. Where there are Arabic or Persian words, or derivations, in this Turkish text these naturally appear in their Turkish form: for example, in the last couplet of Verse 66 the Arabic words are reproduced as *En el Hāk* as in modern Turkish, rather than *An 'al-Haqq*. Where I have incorporated such words directly into my English text, I have used an English spelling which reproduces the Turkish sound in the most convenient way for a reader who may not be familiar with details of the modern Turkish alphabet such as, for example, that the letter 'C' is actually pronounced as a 'J'. I also felt it would be helpful to show, by way of a mark, the fact that a vowel has been lengthened: for example *Hāk* (above) and *mihrāb* (Verse 103). Where a word has passed into English I have used the everyday spelling (*Koran* rather than *Qur'an*). And for words which, while not so commonly used in English, have found their way into the dictionaries, I have used the common dictionary spelling: so, *houri* (Verse 20). Similarly I have used the

English version of names such as Solomon (rather than Suleyman) and Joseph (rather than Yusuf). As between *Muslim* and *Moslem*, both being current (though the latter possibly rather more old-fashioned), I have preferred *Moslem*. It reads better in Verse 153; and I have retained it throughout for consistency.

An aspect of translating from Turkish which calls for comment is that the third person singular in Turkish makes no distinction between the sexes. When, as so often, in my English version, Yunus is seen to talk of 'He who ...' (among many examples see Verse 20), he uses a grammatical form which comprehends both men and women. I have sometimes managed to achieve the effect of the Turkish (for example at the second line of the second couplet of Verse 70) but I regret not having succeeded in every case.

It will be seen that every Verse (save one) ends with the introduction by Yunus, often by invocation, of his name. This is a convention commonly followed by Sufi poets and is not unique to Yunus Emre. It will also be noted that very often, in addressing himself, Yunus changes person and tense. This is not an aberration on the translator's part but, as I conceive it, an aspect of the Sufi comprehension of the nature of time and the unity of existence.

There are also some interesting biblical similitudes: for example in Verse 120.

A word now to academics in the Turkish language – scholars of the word. All readers of Yunus know that the poems often contain several strands, or levels, of meaning. Some derive from actual ambiguities of words or usage: for instance, *devlet* meaning both a 'realm' and also 'prosperity' or, 'good fortune'; and *nefes* meaning either 'breath' – often with the connotation of 'blessing' – or a 'spell', or even in some Sufi Orders a particular poetic form. Some multi-layered meanings arise from words capable of use in a special sense: for example *eren* as explained in the Glossary, or *meydan* meaning both an open space or area – hence 'arena' – and also a place where drink (*mey*) is found. So also some grammatical constructs may be interpreted in several ways, in language which can be extremely terse and compact. There can be no claim to absolute certainty of what constitutes the strictly 'correct' sense of such texts, and I make no such claim for myself. I have made it my rule ultimately to let my heart guide my head for, as the reader will see, it is to the heart that Yunus speaks. To me, a purely intellectual approach to this poetry would be identical to that of the theologians not infrequently reproached by Yunus. He does not criticize their learning as such – he could hardly do that while having regard to the Prophet's injunction to 'seek learning be it as far as in China' – but he does ask them to let into their knowledge the life-giving spirit of love, tolerance and humility.

# INTRODUCTION

Although Yunus Emre's words are essentially timeless, I feel it might still be helpful for a reader not familiar with the time and world in which he wrote to catch at least a glimpse of them. I give below, therefore, a brief paragraph on Yunus himself followed by a thumbnail sketch of the circumstances of the period in which he lived, and the barest outline of the mystical tradition of which his poetry is a part.

Yunus Emre (the two syllables of the second name have equal value) was a Turkish villager who lived about seven hundred years ago and who died around 1320. Little is known with certainty of his life. In the book containing the texts from which I have worked (published in Turkey in 1961), Professor Abdülbâki Gölpınarlı writes that (my translation) 'apart from the traditional accounts and stories about him we have virtually no knowledge of Yunus's life.' Professor Gölpınarlı recounts several endearing legendary tales which have been passed down, often by word of mouth, about this man who is widely revered in Turkey. One fable tells that he left three thousand poems and that these passed into the hands of a certain member of the *Ulema* (Doctors of Theology) named Kasım. This man took the pile of papers to read by a riverside. He read the first poem. 'This does not conform to the *Sher'ia* (Religious Law),' he observed – and flung it into the water. So with the second. And the next. And the next; until a thousand had been despatched. He then started on the remainder. But now he began to burn the discarded poems. One by one he read, and put to the flames, the second thousand. He picked up the next one. Its last couplet read:

Dervish Yunus speak no word untrue – but straightly, from the breast:
For after you a Mullah Kasım comes to put you to the test.

Kasım, astonished, ceased his destruction and reverently preserved the remaining poems. Since then, those thrown into the river have

1

been recited by the fishes of the deep; those burnt, by the birds of the air; and those preserved, by us humans.

Professor Gölpınarlı also gives references to Yunus from various old documents, including the *Vilâyetnâmé* of Haji Bektash (the founder of the Bektashi Order of Dervishes, and a contemporary of Yunus), in which Yunus is stated to have been born at Sarıyer in north-western Anatolia where 'he was a man of poverty who sowed and reaped.' There are however many places in Turkey where the people claim Yunus lies buried.

For me the man is his poetry. His spirit spoke through that poetry, and speaks still; and that spirit is not located in time or space.

By the middle of the thirteenth century, when Yunus was born, the greater part of what is now Turkey had for some two hundred years been effectively under the control or direct rule of the Seljuk Turks. By origin the Seljuks were nomads from the area around the Aral Sea who, with other Turkic peoples, had populated those regions which today remain Turkic-speaking (the Kirghiz, Kazakh, Turkmen and Uzbek republics of the Soviet Union, and the Uighur-inhabited west of the Chinese Republic). In the second half of the eleventh century they had spread out into the north of the Indian sub-continent, Persia, and northern Arabia. By the third decade of that century they had taken the renowned lands of Khorasan, and in 1055 under Tughrūl Bey they were masters of the capital of the Islamic Caliphate, Baghdad, where Harūn ar-Rashid (the Caliph of The Thousand and One Nights) had ruled some two hundred years earlier.

In 1071 at Malazgırt, to the north of Lake Van in the far east of modern Turkey, a battle was fought which was to be as decisive for the future of that part of the world as the Battle of Hastings had been five years earlier for western Europe. At Malazgırt the Seljuks overwhelmed the Byzantine army, took the Byzantine emperor prisoner, and moved into the Anatolian plateau. Seljuk rule was enlightened, and the reigns of Tughrūl's immediate successors, Ālp Arslān and Malik Shah, saw a flowering of the arts, especially of architecture. The chief minister of these two rulers, Nizām ul-Mulk, was the patron of Omar Khayyam whose quatrains (*rub'aiyyāt*) in FitzGerald's translation are so familiar to the English-speaking world.

By the twelfth century those Seljuks who had, after Malazgırt, made Anatolia their home, established their capital at Konya, the Iconium of the Roman Empire and the New Testament. Virtually the whole of Asia Minor was incorporated into the Seljuk Sultanate of Rūm (= Rome, the Eastern Roman Empire). It was during the reign of Ālā ed-Din Keykubād (1219–1236) that the glory of this Sultanate reached its zenith. It was a time of magnificence, but also a time when refugees were bringing foreboding news of the advancing Tartars who had moved outwards from the Mongolian steppes and were now devastating the lands occupied two centuries earlier by the Seljuks. In 1258, Hulaghu Khan, grandson of the great Jenghiz Khan and brother to Kublai Khan (the ruler of China at whose Court Marco Polo was shortly to sojourn), took Baghdad and destroyed the Abbasid Caliphate. This awesome event had a comparable effect on the Moslem world to that on the Roman world wrought by the sack of Rome by the Goths under Alaric in AD 410 – the same sense which found expression in St Augustine's *De Civitate Dei*, one of desolation and a belief that the world as it had hitherto been known had passed away. The Tartar flood lapped up to, and overflowed, the eastern borders of the Sultanate of Rūm. The state endured until the early years of the fourteenth century, but it eked out the last part of its existence as a vassal of the Tartars; and on its western marches another Turkish clan was coming to power under the leadership of Osman, the eponymous founder of the dynasty which was to rule the Ottoman Empire. This was the era in which Yunus Emre lived.

In the atmosphere of insecurity and dread which pervaded the Seljuk lands in the second half of the thirteenth century people were, as always in times of stress and tribulation, particularly open to the sense of the transitory nature and mystery of human existence. But in Islam there had also been a very long tradition of mysticism, going back to the time of the Prophet Mohammed himself. This tradition has been transmitted through Brotherhoods or Orders of mystics (Sufis), and often expressed in poetry.

Possibly the most famous poetry written in this tradition is the *Mesnevi* (the Turkish form of the Persian *Masnavi*) by Jelāl ed-Din Rūmi (that is, Jelāl ed-Din of the land of Rūm) who lived from 1207 to 1273. He was born in Balkh, in what is now northern Afghanistan, but as a child accompanied his father when the family fled from the advancing Tartars. They settled in the Seljuk capital of Konya where Rūmi spent the rest of his life and where his tomb

and shrine still exist. The Sufi Order known as the Mevlevi (from
the title Mevlāna, 'our master', applied to Rūmi) was founded in his
memory some time after his death during the time of his son. This
is the Order sometimes known as the 'whirling dervishes' from the
outward form of their ceremonies. There is no evidence or tradition that Yunus was ever a disciple of Rūmi, but his own poetry
attests that he served that discipleship elsewhere:

> And in those lands to which we came, bearing in our hearts delight,
> We spread abroad to all the message of Taptūk, praise be to God.
>
> We were a servant in the hearth and doorway of Taptūk's abode;
> Poor Yunus, then raw flesh, has now been made true food, praise be to
>     God.                                              (Verse 104)

Nevertheless Yunus is sometimes thought to have sat at the feet of
Rūmi, and some think that the couplet at Verse 24 is a reference to
such a meeting:

> Since when our master, Sovereign Lord, bestowed his loving gaze on
>     us,
> That look of beauty has become for us the mirror of our hearts.

The earthly head of each dervish Order is its Sheykh who, in the
capacity of spiritual mentor, attracts postulants to himself. Yunus
himself did not found an Order:

> Found not a dervish home, O Yunus, thinking that more ears will hear
>                                                       (Verse 99);

yet his influence has been profound, within and outside the Orders.
He spoke, and speaks, to all. It was he who inaugurated the
composition of mystical verses not in the literary language of his
time but in the plain Turkish of the population at large. His poetry
had a strong appeal to the ordinary people of the Turkish-speaking
lands of his lifetime, and that appeal has endured to the present
day. Yunus Emre was, and is, a poet – and a man – of the people.

> Let Yunus ever be remembered when we meet in friendliness.
>                                                       (Verse 18)
> Eternal life, my soul, is this: to leave a name for kindliness. (Verse 44)

# YUNUS EMRE'S
# VERSES
# OF
# WISDOM AND LOVE

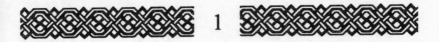

# 1

We need to serve a King Who never may be driven from His throne;
To rest within a place which we may ever feel to be our own.

A bird we need to be, to fly, to reach the very rim of things
To drink that cordial whose drunkenness we never may disown.

We need to be a diving bird, to plunge into the waters' flow;
We need a gemstone to recover such as jewellers cannot know.

To enter in a garden, there to wander in contentment's shade;
To pass the summer as a rose – a rose whose petals never fade.

Mankind must lover be, must ever search to find the true Beloved;
Must burn within the flame of Love – nor burn in any other flame.

Yunus, in stillness hold yourself, to Majesty now turn your gaze
And such a one from self bring forth as shall not come on earth again.

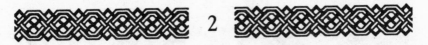

# 2

What wondrous, wondrous thing – which hurt and separation brings to me,
Yet soul intoxicates – this Love? The Poison its own Remedy!

All they torn by distress, let them seek here the antidote most sure;
My pain is salved, my suffering itself is now become my cure.

If you hold out the fire of Love – for the repose of human hearts,
The darkness then is truly light – nor torch nor lantern bright for me.

A thousand times a day the Four Books[1] read which came to earth from Heaven;
If you the brethren[2] yet deny, the Face of Love you cannot see.

Yunus, be not haughty with them – but as dust beneath their feet;
From earth we all have sprung; a bed of roses and the dust still meet.

 **3**

As I travelled, by the wayside stood a mighty, spreading tree,
So graceful and so delicate, my heart said: 'Speak a mystery.'

Where is meaning in such growth when all the world must pass away?
Abundance is to all a sign: turn from it to frugality.

While grace like this adorns the earth, and loveliness bedecks the world,
And hearts of men turn Godward, why then is desire, and wherefore need?

The tree grows old, its time runs out, a bird 'lights briefly on a bough;
And yet on you no bird can find repose – nor dove, nor bird of prey.

To you will come the day when you shall be laid low; your prime now hid,
Your branches feed the fire to heat the boiling pot, the glowing grid.

Yunus, perceive, though you are one your lack is hundred thousandfold:
But take direction from a tree to go rejoicing on your way.

 **4**

Make fantasy that you possess the world entire, from pole to pole:
That you have played the highest stake and won the world's prosperity;

Conceive yourself as Solomon in glory seated on his throne,
That your command can wholly sway the world of demons, peris, all;[3]

Suppose that to the treasure trove of Feridūn and Nūshirvān
You have addition made of all that wealth which Ka'ārūn once enjoyed;

The world imagine as a morsel to be savoured meltingly,
And then suppose it to be fully ready now to be gulped down;

Suppose that life itself is as an arrow in a tight-drawn bow,
And that the taut-held string has been released by you, the arrow flown;

It is as though you struggled in the sea, the water at your throat:
Thresh though you will – to no avail: think now that you are overwhelmed.

With every moment of our breath the contents of life's purse grow less;
Believe that when the half of it is gone you have consumed the whole!

Yunus, if years in hundreds, full of joys, be yours before your death,
Call to mind what you forget – the end of all comes with a breath.

 5

Love our prayer leads,[4] the heart our congregation;
The face of Friendship[5] gives direction,[6] ceaseless the prayer.

The visage of the Friend dispels Duality;
And so the Law must ever stand without the door.

The soul prostrates itself when turned towards the Friend;
Silent the prayer it makes as it bows down to earth.

No other time is like to that of silent prayer;
By us the choice is made of Friend and quietude.

The fivefold times of prayer[7] become for us as one;
When they in five divide – who is it may abide?

To none do we oppose the faith that guides their steps;
As faiths fulfilment find so Love again is born.

Our comrades say to us: 'Abandon not the rule;'
But rule is made for those who follow faithlessly.

A moment past in time we affirmation gave;[8]
That moment, and now this, are for all ages one.

Our prosperous realm, our state, exists in brethren's breath;
By this we have been saved from gross rebelliousness.

Those who wait on Truth at Friendship's open gate,
In certainty they there will find the God-like state.

Yunus a captive stands beside that very gate;
His hope – never to find freedom from that fate.

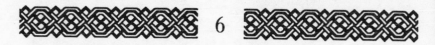 

If you of lovers race, religion, ask – what need does creed fulfill?
The lover is made desolate: of this he can no sense distil.

The lover's heart, the lover's eyes, they turn to the Beloved alone;
Ascetics, pedants – these are rooted most in forms of otherness.

Pious in the hope of Heaven, faith-less forswearing hell as fate,
From each but separates himself. In this sign solely know your state:

The one who truly loves the Friend must always follow where He guides;
And service to the Friend fulfilment finds, and freedom from all care.

Who, like him, to others truthful news can bring of the Beloved?
Not hosts of angels – no, not Gabriel himself: such is the sign.

He will no judgement see who finds no Day of Judgement in each hour;
Munkir and Nekir questions lack when you abandon all desire.

When 'being' and 'non-being' you discard, you know not wish – nor fear;
Science and striving have no more a place; no more are scales,[9] or bridge.[10]

The concourse of the Day of Judgement terror brings to slaves alone;
May you, O Yunus, and all lovers, never know that day of awe.

 7

I came one morning on a burial ground – and there I saw the dead:
Solitary, each one having lost life's road, now lying there.

Nearer I drew, more close to them, and then I saw death's awefulness;
Valiant youths, hopes unfulfilled, unsatisfied, now lying there.

Food for worm and carrion, bodies ravaged by all creeping things,
The young who died before their prime, frost-struck roses, lying there.

Flesh now fast held in death's trap, their souls attain at last to Truth;
O you, whose turn is nigh upon you, see you not these now lying there?

Fallen the teeth which once were pearl, gone the gleaming, golden hair;
But ended the torture of the brain for those in dark damp lying there.

Fled is the shining of their eyes for naught abides that they hold dear;
A single-sheeted shroud alone surrounds these bones now lying there.

Yunus, if you true lover are, be drawn not to possessions' charms:
Who once those charms had known are now become but dark earth lying there.

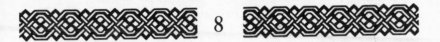 8

I saw, as through the earth I journeyed, men of all nations now laid low;
The mighty and the humble of all generations, now laid low.

Warriors some, and other great men, Vezirs, Teachers of the Word;
Dark night their days are now become, such multitudes like these laid low.

The road before them straightly ran, the pen was ever in their hand;
As sweet as nightingale their tongue: philosophers of might laid low.

Great and small – and both knew tears; fighters who in battle fell;
Broken the bow they once had bent, the shattered arrow now laid low.

Their horses' hooves dust clouds had raised as once they moved to sound of drums;
These Lords whose word had once been law throughout these lands are now laid low.

While yet the little children's voices sang like to the nightingale
Their mothers, separated from them, wait too, in their graves, laid low.

Their fingers henna-dyed, with sweet-lipped slaves they were surrounded once,
Slim as a lance, complexioned as the rose, these ladies now laid low.

The arms of all are folded now, their hopes from God alone derived;
Some, maid-attended, girls with yet a husband's face to see, laid low.

His own state Yunus understands not – God it is brings him to speech;
Their rounded faces paled – how many fresh young brides are here laid low!

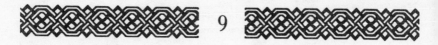 

This world in which we live is like a mighty, huge metropolis;
And in it our short lives are passed as in a teeming market place.

Whoever journeyed to this city only briefly found abode,
And our road homeward whence we came shall never know our tread again.

The first taste of this city's life we find delicious, honey-sweet;
Then see the latter bitterness – like to the venom of the snake.

Between competing loveliness the heart at first seeks one to seize;
Yet in the latter days these but repel – like a deceitful crone.

This city's foolish fantasies are without bounds, are numberless;
A heedless, grazing herd are they whom images like this entice.

The city has a Ruler Whose benevolence is for each one,
And they who come to know Him find existence where before was none.

The one who knows his own worth truly he has fathomed his own state;
With Love he now discerns himself as one in early days of Spring.

See poor Yunus, who in suffering feels yet reverential awe
Which makes as sweet as honey, sugar, every breath which he may draw.

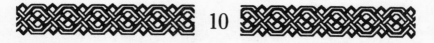 10

Knowledge true is found in learning – true knowledge is to know your self;
And if that self you have not learned your reading has been all for naught.

The end of reading – what is it? That man may come to know the Truth.[11]
Save that you to Truth are led your reading is of nothing worth.

Then say not: 'I have read, have learned,' or: 'I obeyed the rules of faith;'
If you perceive not Man as Truth your efforts have been wasted breath.

The meaning of the Fourfold Book[12] a single letter [13] can enfold;
If you that letter cannot tell – what point your reading time untold?

Recite a twenty-nine syllabic line, faultless from end to end;
When you that letter speak, O Master, can you make its meaning known?

Yunus Emre's word is this to masters: 'Mount, if so you must,
And travel thousand times on Hāj – but lodging in a heart is best.'

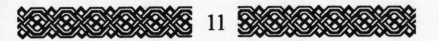 11

The instant I prostrate myself in prayer my Moon is newly born;
Each moment festival becomes for me; Summer and Winter – Spring.

The brilliance of that Moon no shadow sees from any passing cloud;
Forever full, it never wanes, from earth gives radiance to the skies.

Its gleaming light all darkness scatters from the confines of my heart;
How may both darkness and such radiance find place together there?

It was on earth I saw my Moon: why in the sky need I then be?
My gaze I will turn earthward whence compassion ever flows to me.

Though I speak not of Moon or Sun a word for lovers will suffice;
If I tell not what I have loved, the pain of Love will stifle me.

If Yunus then has loved, what of it? Many are they who Truth have loved;
And Truth said these will inward burn – and so to It my head is bowed.

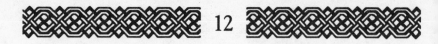 

My heart's abode! How comes it overflowing from the lands of Love?
Though head high I may walk, yet from that head the streams of Love still flow.

How do I speak my mystery, and tell what should be told to none?
Dissolves my patience, my resolve, when Friendship makes Its presence known.

Can he in patient silence stand who has the Face of Friendship seen?
From inner turmoil speaks the one who cries: 'I saw the Face of Truth.'

The Beloved is made manifest in colours multitudinous –
But one is His accent which a hundred thousand hearts with joy has filled.

My life together with the Friend is like to the sun in swirling cloud;
Moments there are His Face is veiled – then, see, His beauty is revealed!

Is it then strange that now poor Yunus is in Love to such excess?
Than Love there is no thing to be preferred – It is Its own success.

The Truth a heart bestowed on me which, in an instant, falls to awe;
A breath – and it knows happiness; a breath – and it is filled with tears.

A breath there comes when you could think it frozen, cold as Winter's depth;
A breath – and born of beauty new a fruitful vineyard it becomes.

There comes a breath when it can speak no more, nor any word expound;
A breath – and words of pearl pour from its tongue, balm for the grieving soul.

A breath when it ascends to Heaven then sinks to depths of earth again;
Again a breath – it to a droplet shrinks, or as a torrent overflows.

A breath when it in ignorance abides, can nothing comprehend;
A breath – it into Wisdom plunges and with every sage unites.

Another breath when, in a ruined scape, a demon it becomes;
A breath – with Belkis it soars up, ruler of spirits and of men.

A breath – and it, within the mosque, in reverent prayer prostrates itself;
A breath – and, Bible pages reading, it becomes a cloistered monk.

A breath – and Jesus-like the dead themselves it brings again to life;
A breath – and, one with Pharaoh and Hamān,[14] enters the house of pride.

A breath, and it is Gabriel become, brings mercy as friends meet;
A breath, and it has lost its way – and Yunus lost in wonderment.

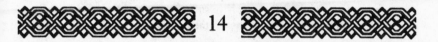 14

O comrades, hear it told to you that Love is as a shining sun;
The heart which never Love has known is but a hard unyielding stone.

What from a stony heart can spring? Venom breathes from lips of such;
However soft the speech, the words are as the clash of battlefield.

The truly loving heart, it softens in the flame like candlewax;
But stony hearts in darkness dwell, as hardest Winter are – and fierce.

Before the portal of the Lord, attendant on His majesty,
An ever watchful serjeant of the guard, there stands the lovers' star.

Leave aside all care, poor Yunus; abandon art if this must be;
The saint's need first is Love: no difference will you in the dervish see.

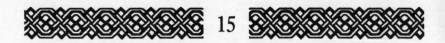 

If for God's sake my soul feels pain, it is enough to wait on Him;
Can there be anguish greater than a separation from Your Face?

The world is witness to the flame of Love which burns within my breast;
As scent which smoke sends out gives of the presence of the fire a trace.

The warrior of Love laid waste the regions where my heart has dwelled;
My soul he captive took and, like a Tartar foe, he brought me low.

Should any work ill deeds, the Sultan's slaves in duty rigid stand;
Their fate is to be disciplined – or in the market put on show.

Yunus, make not complaint that you have suffering known because of Love;
All that is needful for the lovers comes to them from the Beloved.

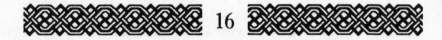 16

Tell, my tongue, that Love bedews my face;
My heart, my eyes, with Love are overflowing.

Its smoke dawn-breezes wafting to the skies,
My body like the wood of aloes burning.

What chain-mail stands against Your fiery Love?
Its arrow pierces, sinks into the soul.

If I should leave these waters I must die:
Fish-like I have my Being in Your bowl.

In my own tongue my Lord's name I recite;
He orders me to come, to wait on Him.

Are those who love You reckoned with the wise?
Mad every moment – if one instant sane!

Yunus, on sainthood's Road be dust in flight;
A stage upon that Road is Heaven's height.

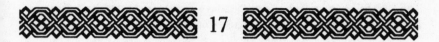 17

What can *those* know of this Love who sleep in sloth?
And how set out upon the Road who have no food?

Let us away, to look upon the Beautiful,
The radiance of Whose Face can famished thousands fill.

Since Love is seen today beyond the tavern door,
What shall they say who with such colours paint the pure?

From angels' mountains, gardens of the blest, he strays –
From immortality itself – who counts his days.

Then throw away the 'We', the 'Other' let us be;
Who sense the Unity put off Duality.

Yunus, be *one*: become the secret in the heart,
In that of which the dervish mystery is part.

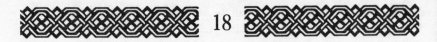 

Within the vision of the saints put not your piety on sale;
Make not by faith addition of hypocrisy to Love unfeigned.

The Law[15] as combless honey is – the Path[16] as butter well refined;
But why, for Friendship's sake, may these two not in sweetness be combined?

The false will never yield his own; the true will give, nor count what's due;
It is in vain to think the false can ever be conjoined with true.

He the Koran bestowed on us Who has His home in every heart;
That heart knows not the Owner of its home which takes not Adam's part.

The first man went astray when he, in Heaven, ate of certain seed;
Let those who are at one with God hold never to the Devil's deed.

If you look on the True what shall It instantly bring to your eye?
Sell not the Meaning of the saints to those who have no will to buy.

Accept that you unknowing are, yet from the One who knows receive;
Prolong not discourse, adding word to word, but go upon your way.

The word you speak let it be sweet, your actions filled with loveliness:
Let Yunus ever be remembered when we meet in friendliness.

Break, my love-torn heart – see what they do to you;
Among this people many look on us to mock.

Then let them laugh, and jeer that Truth is not with us;
We love Truth still – although the heedless see this not.

Long is the Road, and many the stages to be reached:
No easy defiles, deep the torrents to be crossed.

Knowingly we took this Road, in throes of Love;
Yet some contend that into exile we were driven!

He who would contend, let him come manfully
Into the open field – who has the skill for this.

But Yunus, seek not here to find a place of strife;
Within the drinking place are manly ones enough!

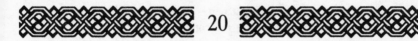 20

My Friend, the arrow of Your Love will safely glance off hearts of stone;
Yet he who by that Love is struck, the wound in heart and head is one.

His tears flow day and night, unceasing, made a lover by Your Love;
But he whose only care is You, perplexity will no more own.

For those who fall in Love with You, their hearts compassionately burn;
The one who gives himself to You from every toil finds his return.

A poisoned banquet is prepared for lovers of mere worldliness;
But those who heed the latter end pass safely by the venomous.

Whose mind is rightly set will not be influenced by recompense;
And thoughts of paradisal houris' flashing eyes tempt not his sense.

True Lover – be of those who waste not soul to win a place in space;
Thousands the wounds of those who Friendship barter in the marketplace.

For the wise this world is as a thing imagined, like a dream;
By self-surrender to You we find freedom from such fantasies.

With Love of Truth the heart and eyes of Yunus brim and overflow;
Who loving discourse chooses moves beyond the bounds of friend and foe.

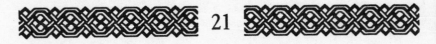
The brotherhood of Truth came not to understanding in ill-deeds;[17]
Vitality of Truth comes not to being in hypocrisy.

The Truth an ocean is, the Law[18] a ship which has its Being there;
And many on the ship embark who of the waters nothing share;

As many to a gate draw nigh and, having come, await without
Though they might pass within – a place to them of mystery, and doubt.

The children of the Law make disputation – argument their Lord;
The brotherhood of Truth will never rest content with barren word.

Who of the Four Books exposition makes – rebels, leaves Truth behind;
The one whose reading is but commentary the substance will not find.

Yunus, put to death the self, if on the Path you are embarked;[19]
Who do not kill the self in Truth are by eternity unmarked.

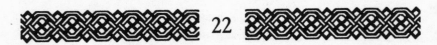
O lovers, would you know where you in Truth may find the brotherhood?
But look – when you have need the brethren ready stand – have always stood.

To those who know not Love my words are but an echo off the rock;
And they who have no spark of Love in wastelands of the mind yet walk.

Be never false to anyone, tell never any lie to Love;
For those who speak lies *now*, will *then* find there is but imprisonment;

O you who do not know yourself,[20] who find no meaning in the Word;
If you Truth's Being seek, It is in Knowledge – and in the Koran.

Love's Being God has given, and still gives, to him who says 'I am;'
In whom is but a particle of Love, there too is God's own self.

Many are they who say to Yunus: 'Senile one, put Love aside;'
But Love in us is newly born and is the ripe fruit of the soul.

 23

In silence strive, for silence is itself the purity of speech:
Words that through effort of the mind are strained will tarnish human hearts.

God's own command it is to speak aright: He said 'Proclaim the Truth;'
And he who falsehood speaks today, tomorrow will be put to shame.

It is not water washes clean this rust which darkens human hearts;
Boldly proclaim the Word which of the Very Word is summary.

He who cannot see creation through the eye of Unity,
However great as teacher his repute, he wars against the Truth.

Then let me speak to you the nature of the Law and of the Truth:
The Law a vessel is and Truth the boundless sea on every side;

Whatever strength that ship may find in timbers stout and firmly built,
The movement of those waters will in time most surely shatter it.

O lover, listen to the inner Word – then speak it to the world;
The misbeliever of the Word of Truth, of mischief is the saint.

For those who in the everlasting world with joy are overflowing,
What is thought, or heart, or intellect – or even life itself?

In every moment we are pupils, Love's instruction book we read;
God Himself the teacher is, and Love His schoolroom of the Self.

Since the day the saints on us bestowed the beauty of their gaze,
What was apportioned as his share to Yunus has its harvest borne.

21

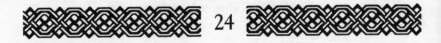 

Those who sainthood would deny are rebels in the way of God;
Who in rebellion find their way are as the rust on human hearts.

The burden of our Love we bore until we came to the Beloved;
That Friend to me is remedy for all my pain and all my hurt.

Before this earth had yet been fashioned, or the firmament been formed,
The homeland of the saints in being *is* – the citadel of God.

Since when our Master,[21] Sovereign Lord, bestowed his loving gaze on us,
That look of beauty has become for us the mirror of our hearts.

Hasan, he of the brethren of the deer,[22] himself the Word pronounced,
But since that Word from God proceeded, who may say the Word was his?

O poor one, rest in poverty, from pride and rancour free yourself;
The wind from all sides passes and repasses – for no-one will it stay.

Reciting, but inditing not, and straying not though he should err;
Yunus! Who understands this Word of Love is meet to understand.

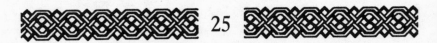 

O Friend, such Love I have for You; Your place is deep inside my breast;
Wondrous Your attributes which neither day nor night can give You rest.

While you can clearly see the rose, stretch not your hand to touch its thorn;
When such a Path before you straightly lies, shall fear from foe suborn?

Those who stand opposed to me make question on what claim I speak;
And I respond – 'What right to question me?' – for I a Master own.

Give that which you have earned or gained to the relief of needy ones;
However long you have to live, know that the latter end is death.

Those who here can see themselves, these travel ever by the Road;
The merest ant[23] I hold in high esteem which on that Road is found.

Though, like the nightingale, my song shall with the dawn each morning cease,
Yet Meaning burgeons as my inner hurt to heavy heart brings peace.

Yunus, let your name be spread afield as lowly as the earth;
Such as is due to the Beloved I own a poverty of heart.

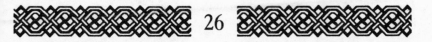 26

O Friend, my heart and head are one within the furnace of Your Love;
But though my heart is in that fire consumed, in that is my delight.

Burning in Your Love, my weeping into laughter is transformed;
To scoffers it is war when tearfully to You I bring my plight.

If I should speak, my Word is soft; my heart, if I speak not, a wound;
Whose words are nothing worth wait everywhere to fling the steady stone.

See now the stones which rain on me, the challenge borne for Friendship's sake;
They strike me to the heart – but those in like condition come to me.

These are they who know our state, for who of them can Love deny?
The Truth it is we love – the people only surface beauty see.

This for the saints did not suffice, they did not tarry on the Road;
To those who truly love the Truth the whole world is a brotherhood.

Poor Yunus, your true essence grasp – to Friendship open wide your eyes;
Look from whichever Zodiac tower, upon Him yet the sun's light lies.

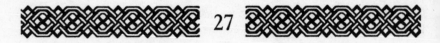 

This city of real Being, how I long each day to enter in
And, being there, to see the glory of my Sultan's Face within.

For though His voice comes ever to me I have here no sight of Him;
My life I willingly would give if I could only glimpse that Face.

Within that Sultan's private rooms are seven places of retreat;
Would that I might at each of these, in turn, find for my soul a place.

Before each gate a sentinel; a hundred thousand at command;
Girded, I long to seize the sword of Love and put them all to flight.

The Leylā of Mejnün am I; and lover of the Merciful;[24]
I would the Face of my Beloved see – so would that I were mad.

The Friend has come to us as guest, time without number, year on year;
I would that I might be for Him, like Ismaïl, a sacrifice.[25]

Earth into jewels is transformed when saints their gaze bestow on it;
Could I be but the dust in which the footsteps of the saints have trod.

Poor Yunus is, as all, by nature's fourfold elements sustained;
I yearn to be within the mystery of Love and life contained.

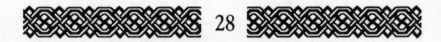 

O you who say that I am good, know that I am the worst of all –
That felons are less fell than I: upon the Road so much I fall.

If there be slave more culpable than I, then go and search him out;
The Word of Wisdom on my lips – within still longing for this world.

Though honoured with the name of Sheykh I have forsaken piety;
The self I have indulged; can I now hope to bargain with the Truth?

My robe is but a veil for all my faults; my care is wrongly set;
Though mystic Word is on my tongue, my heart engaged in commerce yet.

Those to whom I guidance gave, I saw that they to Truth attained;
But all my counsel to myself effect for me has never gained.

Of good repute in sight of men, my heart is only falsely true;
Baghdad itself could not contain a greater charlatan than you.

Friendly without, within a foe; sweet-tongued, my heart a renegade;
Where name and deed are so opposed – was ever falsity so made?

Such is my state: to outward sight afire yet cold and raw within –
Advancing not a step along the Road, from Heaven I tidings bring!

Yunus's fame is spread abroad, yet culpable his piety;
And still it seems my Lord's benevolence that fault shall yet forgive.

 29

Who comprehends the Word, a single word his face may make to shine;
The seasoned Word may cause to prosper all the works of him who speaks.

A word can be the tumult's end, can bring the blinded mind to see;
A word may into oil and honey sweet transform a poisoned dish.

So weightily pronounce your word, that so the unworthy be bemused;
Your word speak with propriety – drop never an unseemly word.

Come, my brother, O majestic one, come, hearken to my word;
The thousand jewels of the lover's face a word can make black earth.

Walk then, walk the Way, but let not knowledge make you unaware;
Be watchful – with a single heedless word your tongue may sear a soul.

O Yunus, from the plenitude of words speak that which should be said;
Take heed, a word alone may separate you from the line of Sheykhs.

Not one there is who understands us, nor our effort and our toil;
Not lust for wealth, nor place, our Being rules – not self our soul's employ.

We seek not to reproach another's state, we will not jeer or mock;
We come not to deny the world, not are we of the Christian cross.

But we the essence of these still have known, and of this world remain;
Though not for self is our desire in this our journey through that world.

Then Yunus says: 'O sovereign mine, for me there is another Lord;
The gold and silver of this world forsake – no place we have in dross.'

This heart of mine; what may I make of this which will not stay with me?
Once it had seen the Lover's Face, it counsel gives – but none receives.

For sake of God, O righteous ones, give back to me this heart of mine;
Once it had sojourned with the Friend, no more will it bow down to me.

How may I pass my life in harmony with such a heart as this,
Which in the wilderness abandoned me, nor sends to know my state?

While it still journeyed by my side I gave to piety its due;
Now broken, shattered, all my schemes; now humbled, powerless, am I.

Within, beside the Friend, my heart – while I stand weeping at the door;
Were thousand times a thousand sorrows mine, it asks not why I grieve.

If I cry out: 'O heart of mine, what of the dues religion claims?'
It makes reply: 'Be not confused – Love is not reached by works alone.'

And should I make to harness it with: 'Pay the burden of your dues;'
Plunging and rearing it reproaches me and cries: 'You see not Truth.'

If you be faithful to your word, of all mouths blessed is your mouth;
Though I repeat this an eternity *its* ear hears not my voice.

And yet my heart, and yet my soul, two that are fashioned but as one,
A thousand times abandon Yunus, he to Friendship's Face still turns.

 32

What grief is this, O God, which finds not any cure?
And what this hurt, this pain – a wound no eye can see?

My heart, bereft of joy, finds no satiety;
And still to Love it turns – but gives no heed to me.

And when it turns to me, its counsel freely gives:
'The heart that burns with Love, from Love finds no release.'

The love that clings to soul – this is not any Love;
Who casts not soul aside sees not the Loved One's Face.

In that Love's marketplace where souls are set for sale,
My soul is put on view – but buyer there is none.

Love has a human face; and what is of this world
It will not set at naught – nor fear of the Latter Day.

For still this world of ours is with that Latter one;
The lover owns a place, though this is known to none.

'The lover now has died,' we hear the prayer pronounced;
What dies is animal – true Lovers perish not.

My Lord, if you be wise, be steadfast on your Way;
Here it begins, here ends – its worth unquestioned flows.

The place of brotherhood is nobler than the heavens –
No polo-ball is seen, though stick delivers blows!

The gateway of the saints, of magnanimity:
All they who come in Truth will never be denied.

Into this Unity is Yunus now absorbed;
The compass of his mind cannot conceive return.

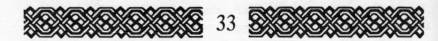

We need the Vision true – not what the world reveals;
We need that Meaning which contention cannot yield.

The blessed Night of Power[26] this very night can be;
The morrow put aside, no need of dawn have we.

Let us but take a single sip from Love's cup here,
And we forsake the heavenly waters of Kevser.

So of that brimming cup let us now drink a draught:
The drunkenness it gives can bring no after-pain.

Yunus fell intoxicated in the Way;
He has no need of shame invoking Taptūk's name.

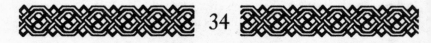

Of such who claim the dervish name, whom dervish-hood has caught with joy,
The hearts are unconfined – there is no more for them the fear of shame.

Humility is theirs – a silent tongue replies to him who rails,
No blow for blow returned; so from the people they are separate.

Hold from the crowd some way apart, and drive all turmoil from your heart;
A hundred thousand for the dervish are as one – and none a foe.

The whole world is your friend, O dervish, if you truly dervish be;
What passes bounds make temperate – that there be no more enmity.

In this our world of dervish-hood our treasury is poverty;
And naught save that do we desire – not home, not wealth, not property.

If you have held another's hand, or heart bestowed on fellow man –
When you confess *that* faith, you never shall know infidelity.

Yunus, once you have seen a Man, think not the One to multiply:
Make no distinction, 'this' or 'that'; the dervish casts no wits awry.

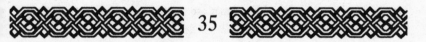 35

Our country is from others set apart, no land like this to see:
In credal book is not set out our faith, nor our theology.

This way of our belief indeed is known to multitudes of men;
In this or latter world you will not find through books our ways of praise.

The outward cleansing matters not; nor ritual of hand and foot;
And even when our head is not bowed down our prayer we raise up still.[27]

Not in Mecca is our trust, nor yet in mosque or formal prayer;
In Truth, in silent Truth, we pray unceasing to that Truth alone.

But still to Mecca let us turn, still make ablution as of old,
And enter still the house of prayer; these mark us yet as incomplete.

Your fellow by your deed is hurt – though pure ablution's water be;
Know well that it is by God's grace, and that alone, if clean are *we*.

Who penetrates another's Word? This state outruns the mind of man;
And these – our Moslem renegades? Tomorrow, *there*, for all to see!

Yunus, make new that soul in you, that so your Friendship be recalled;
If you with Love give ear, Our power you share to all eternity.

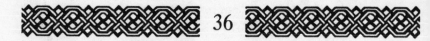 

This people call me Sufi: ceaselessly I ply my rosary;
My heart will not accept the Wisdom which my tongue forever tells.

Though licensed[28] to expound the Word, my piety is but a fraud;
For all my care is elsewhere placed, the Way ahead veiled from my sight.

My words are wise, and yet I know they are a garment as for show;
Not to heart's poverty I turn – pride holds its place still in my heart.

A dervish I, indeed! My patience spent, my tongue denies the Truth;
The words I daily din into my ear my inner self heeds not.

They kiss my hand who see me, look upon my dervish cap and robe
And make an image of me as of one without the stain of sin.

My worship, superficiality; pleasant my words of cheer;
Could they but see my inner trade – a trickster of ten thousand years.

The people see a Sufi face; they greet me, stand aside in awe;
Were I to do as they suppose, my strength would fail, hand reach no more.

To outward eye, a dervish I: yet hollow, sweet though my word might be;
Yet even he who has forsworn his faith is not so base as me.

Yunus, commit your failings to your God, to Him your all entrust;
He will not deal with you as you have done: His Grace is full and just.

The Path the brothers travel is far narrower than narrowness;
It was an ant bestrode the road like this of Solomon the King.[29]

The ant found tongue, and to the host of Solomon direction gave;
That ant was moved to speech until response was made by Solomon.

The heart, too, speaks; it welcome seeks, calls: 'Let me quickly come to you.'
Only until it finds the Friend my heart conformist is to me.

No person lives who takes away the burden of another's soul;
Who claims to have the strength for this – let him stretch out his hand and see.

Whatever word one to another speaks, of evil or of good,
From God alone comes its reward: we travel by a narrow Road.

Tear-streaked we see the lover's face; unceasing day and night he weeps;
The lover tears of blood will shed until the Loved One seeks what ails.

The Four Books[30] much I read, and taught their meaning much in parable;
But when I came to learn Love's Truth – I saw all in a syllable.

Such as boast their dervish-hood, who eat not what they may not eat;
Forbidden fruit they will not touch – only while it is out of reach.

'So-and-so has died,' they cry, 'much was the property he left;'
The increase of that property was only while it was possessed.

Two people talked of Yunus, saying: 'Would that we might see that sage.'
Another spoke: 'I saw him once – a lover well beyond his age!'

Turn to me for but an instant; pity show, lift up your veil;
As on the fourteenth night the moon, so gleams the radiance of your face.

The word your mouth lets fall evokes a hundred thousand gratitudes;
Grant that these lips, this tongue, may speak – so I might tell my thankfulness.

Two rows of two-and-thirty pearls in coral set – so are your teeth;
Yet purer they, though like, than pearls; and as for worth, beyond compare.

The pureness of your qualities is wholesome as God's gift of grain;
Your brow, the twin arcs of your eyes put into shade the new moon's light.

As moth may not escape the flame, though seen, so too am I with you;
The glance that lights me from your eyes, twin torches, sears into my soul.

The lover's neck is haltered fast and held by murmurings of Love;
Yet lovers do not seek release – unransomed hostages their fate.

Of which your lovely attributes could tongues unnumbered tell the whole?
God in His mercy grant that you from hurtful eyes may stand afar.

Your slender figure is for me as graceful as a cypress tree;
Self-doubt is all that I can feel when I your ears bejewelled see.

For Yunus the sweet vision of your face vouchsafed a sight of Truth;
How can I tear myself away from what revealed that Truth to me?

O you who read in many books and think me of such little worth,
If you would see the secret clear revealed – read but one page of Love.

Mark not the surface of the word; in action will the choice be seen;
Open the inward eye, and see the face of Love – and the Beloved.

Look well, where lover is there too Beloved will be in ecstasy.
Two in one involved; think not that they are two – nor you apart.

If you are yet locked in Duality, are captive to your mood,
If you the Friend seek not, the jurist snare you have not understood.

If, dervish-robed and girt, to purest Love you give the tribute due,
You would, like Abd ur-Razzāk, pupils, sanctity no more pursue.

A man of God, a noble soul, apostatized, abjured his faith;
Much more need you your idol shatter – body render to the flame.

If you had learned to see yourself, had blotted out the image false
And to the Truth been true, It would unasked reveal Itself in you.

You knew not shame nor fame, elect and common were to you as one;
But if you now have truly learned – then come, and read a page of Love.

From Love this world was born – as Love has brought to tongue these words of
    mine.
Poor Yunus, what then should he know, who never learnt from black on white.

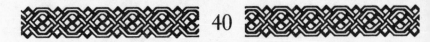 

That by which our heart is held, whole worlds there are which love It too;
To whom should I deny this – claim there is a single gate and Way?

That which is loved of the Beloved, to us must be as well beloved;
The friends of our Friend – how can we be other than at peace with them?

If lover you would truly be, be friend to him who loves your Friend;
And if this be not so with you, you may not claim to be my friend.

He whom you hold of little worth has in the highest rank his place;
Belittle not, accord respect to all; so was the Pathway made.

But if your heart is filled by Love, for all make self a sacrifice;
So may you find your place, a loyal leader[31] in the ranks of Love.

To hearts which truly love the Truth, that Truth will open wide the door;
Put self-regard aside, pull down entire the house of selfishness.

The high and low, both friend and foe, they all are servants of the Friend;
If you would tell this Word abroad, what choice but to forsake your home?

This, the counsel Yunus gives, is as a treasure, secret, hid;
Those who are lovers of the Friend, their selves of both the worlds have rid.

 41

We fell to muse in Meaning's house; from there existence we surveyed;
We found that both the worlds are visible in all that truly is.

The tracing of the skies above, the deepest of the depths below,
The seventy thousand mysteries we found in all that truly is.

The seven earths and seven skies, the mountains and the oceans there,
Hell itself and very Heaven we found in all that truly is.

The black of night and light of day, and in the sky the planets seven,
The Word inscribed on lasting rock, we found in all that truly is.

The Sinai mountain Moses climbed, the angels' Holy House aloft,
The trumpet blast of Israfil, we found in all that truly is.

The Jewish Torah and the Christian Book, the Psalms and the Koran,
The message which they each proclaim, we found in all that truly is.

True is the Word which Yunus speaks: devotion we respect in all;
For where you want Him there, we found, is God – in all that truly is.

 42

Whatever word I speak, of You it is my tongue will ever tell;
Wherever I may walk, it is to You my wishes wing themselves.

Truth it is that those who love You not – they are but lifeless form;
So they who have that life, their need is a beloved one, like You.

By all the world You are beloved, though yet beyond the veil, unseen;
This, and the latter, world by sight of You revealed would be destroyed.

Demons, peris, men and angels, all are lost in Love of You;
In wonder wrapt, before You stand, adoring company of Heaven.

Were I to drink a poisoned chalice from Your hand, yet life it gives;
Though I its Meaning cannot tell, my soul its healing power knows.

Though honey-sweet my food, without You it is poison to my soul;
Where else to taste the savour of the soul that only is in You?

If pain must be my lot, a hundred thousand sufferings my fate,
Still shall my joy not fade – in loving You I count no more the score.

What matters it if Yunus here is but an atom in a world of Love?
They stand, the earth and sky, God's firmament, in virtue of Love's fire.

## 43

How should the stream of life avail, when life we have abandoned now!
To jewellers we have made over gems – all such we have abandoned now.

Not everything of worth is counted valuable to this our band;
Naked we came – the commerce of the world we have abandoned now.

Faithlessness and faith, the two to us are veiled in journeying;
With faithlessness we have reposed – and faith we have abandoned now.

If 'you' and 'I' appear to us, we only know Duality;
We toiled in each of these estates – and both we have abandoned now.

In the marketplace we know, our wealth becomes our poverty;
Our commerce being such, anxiety we have abandoned now.

A pedlar I have been such as no profit ever sought to win,
As profit is not ours to hold – and loss we have abandoned now.

In piety we asked, but none of what we sought fell to our lot;
Since we have now renounced all such, so doubt we have abandoned now.

A hundred thousand years of life, and yet the day has barely dawned;
Through numbers we have passed, the singular we have abandoned now.

Yunus was once much occupied by bounded time and circumstance;
Infinity attaining, time itself we have abandoned now.

## 44

Open your eyes to all my heart, yet let your thoughts be circumspect;
Look to the order of your life, but never to another's fault.

With all, so rule the way you live that they recall we all shall die;
Eternal life, my soul, is this: to leave a name for kindliness.

If you would change the world in which we live into the world to come,
In worship pass your days and nights; recline not, cup in hand, at ease.

Should you a dervish see approach, stoop to his feet in reverence;
If he should ask for alms let not your brow be by resentment knit.

Be careful that the word you speak is given as you heard it first;
Assume not to yourself the wit to add a single word to it.

The world is luscious, sweet, to us – is meet for Man to take and eat;
So what is ill, is harmful, covet not to gnaw in eager greed.

The food five fingers carry to your mouth, gulp not as if your meed;
Cut, put by for those in want, never forget another's need.

Yunus, He Who gave it takes your life when death comes on that day;
Tomorrow you shall see Him – now, from saints' regard turn not away.

 45

Advise not those who know not Love, the loveless heed not your advice;
Without Love we are but as beasts – to beasts advice is mystery.

Stand never from the wise apart, but shun the ways of ignorance;
From meanness God withdraws Himself – the Face of Love such cannot see.

Submerge the dark rock in the water – though you bathe it fifty years
As ever stone will it remain, nor substance change for use by Man.

Yet from the rock rise many waters, at its foot that bounties grow;
Than rock more hard the heart ill-nurtured, never can it fruit bestow.

The great grey owl expends not strength on sparrow-hawk by day or night;
The eyeless mole is its concern, the water-fowl feel not its might.

The falcon, peregrine, and hawk – much praise is theirs from those who praise;
But birds of prey which lose their strength no more are true to raptor's ways.

The dual universe's sun transforms the superficial world;
Those who know not think it dead – by death how can it be defined?

Yunus, be not ignorant like these, but from the wise stand not afar;
If ignorance is joined by faith, the light will pierce the darkened mind.

  46

Souls on the sacrificial Road look not to life's anxiety;
You are the Soul I need, not life full of the world's anxiety.

You are the Soul within all souls, the stream of all created life;
To us You are true faith, belief; far from the creeds' anxiety.

I bathed my wound and, wiping it, I knew whence it had come to me;
The care Love feels for me is other than my wound's anxiety.

Your Love to all has opened me, my grief I keep not to myself;
And now that I have seen You plain, I hide not in anxiety.

May there be any cure for me, when I myself am hurt to Him?
Afflicted, I may come to You – my cure is no anxiety.

Come, let us be lovers, always in that Lover's company;
I laid me down in drunkenness, not there is my anxiety.

The sharply pointed arrow-tip of Love has pierced me to the heart;
But if of Love I die I feel not from that tip anxiety.

What did I do with soul or heart? I threw them on the fire of Love;
Though loyalty I have forgot, I know not doubt's anxiety.

I flew aloft from Love's high tower, and made its circuit as I passed;
I was united with the Friend – and sensed no more anxiety.

I plunged into the oceans' depths; the mother-of-pearl in darkness found;
Myself a gem became; no longer knew the seas' anxiety.

Let where I stand be Sinai's mount, and Lover's Face what I behold,
I need not Moses now – no more the 'you'-and-'I' anxiety.

This Yunus they recalled; they said: 'His caravan has gone its way;'
At journey's end no more for me the caravan's anxiety.

Who travels by true Meaning's way will no more feel despondency;
For hearts which hear true Meaning's voice will never perish utterly.

The flesh will wither, souls die not; that which has gone will not return;
The flesh it is which perishes – souls will not vanish utterly.

Though you a hundred thousand words to hearts unjewelled may address,
Save God give grace to you and them, that grace is absent utterly.

Take care, the heart of Love is brittle crystal; see you break it not;
Once shattered, any hope to make it whole abandon utterly.

If you should leave your pitcher at the well-head for a thousand years,
How may it fill itself? It must stand there alone – and empty, utterly.

Hizir and Ilyās, the two, they both drank of the stream of life;
And in the years long passed they had themselves not perished utterly.

This world was formed by God from naught, in virtue of Mohammed's Love;
Who come into it may not stay, they are not of it utterly.

Yunus, while yet your eyes can see, look well to do what you must do;
Who thence have gone will come no more, have hence departed utterly.

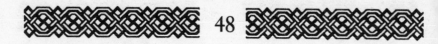 

When you an 'I' pronounce, recall that Meaning does not know that state;
Is ever sentinel with double vision set to guard a gate?

If for yourself you have a care and heed this Word which I pronounce,
Say not of anything you see that you and It are separate.

For It alone abides, beloved in every nation of the world;
It is not in the stars to separate Love from the Beloved.

As you forsake your faithlessness harm not the faith you now pretend;
Hostility is foe to us – yet never stranger, if no friend.

The message brought you by this Word is but abridged, indeed abridged;
Make sainthood for yourself the choice – much more than mere maturity?

Master, this language of the birds is that which Solomon once knew;[32]
Hear me, master, when I tell you this is not mere empty breath.

Looking not to right nor left Yunus and Taptūk speak joy;
Know that the lovers of the Real are wholesome, right, not sinister.

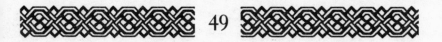
Look not on anyone with scorn, not one there lives devoid of worth;
To look disdainfully was never pleasing to the dervish heart.

Make of your heart itself a dervish, to the Friend yourself be friend;
With heart by Love possessed the dervish never can know emptiness.

A dervish will be known to dervish, steadfast on the Path to Truth;
Like to the phoenix is the dervish, not to kite or bird of prey.

Dervish-hood is of the heart, has passed beyond the dual worlds;
Proclaims the message of the Lord in openness and Love to all.

O Yunus, he who knows the Truth can never speak a word untrue;
Who travels with Duality the rightful Road has yet to view.

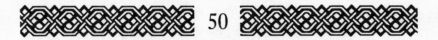
Empty the prayer you make if you have once a human heart destroyed;
The two-and-seventy nations cannot cleanse your hands and face for you.

Countless saints have been and, having left their lands, passed on their Way;
To Truth they all ascended, phoenix-like – the others, lost, astray.

The Road is that which straightly goes; the eye is that which sees the Right;
*He* is the saint who stoops himself; in arrogance there is no sight.

If by the true Path you have passed, have touched the hem of holiness,
Have ever worked for good – one deed is as a thousand, nothing less.

Yunus joins word to word, as though to butter he would honey add;
His goods he hawks, as gems to those who wish to buy – for others, mad.

There is no slave without a Lord, nor is a Lord such with no slave;
How may the Lord be recognized were there no slave to make him known?

Sultans there will always be, and slavery will yet endure;
The Lord alone is everlasting – this the abiding Principle.

From everlasting, God and slave; such is the Road unvarying;
See which slave is, which is God – perceive, who understanding have.

Wrap yourself in Unity, and tell the news of Truth and Joy:
To leave behind Duality, O slave, forsake Identity.

See the hidden sight before you, mystery within the view;
To the slave deliverance descends – not *he* it was who knew.

Tell, tell again – you are the Whole, you are not mere material;
Of Meaning you the image are, entire – find in yourself the Lord.

Come then, take away the veil, flee from self unto the Self;
You, too, will to Mir'āj attain; to you will every path then lead.

O sense, where are you to be found? A single mouth speaks every tongue;
Each piece of the connected Whole brings tidings of the Total Mind.

See, Yunus, where your Being is; not on earth, nor in the skies;
Await, the curtain now unfolds; come now, and bow in reverence.

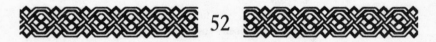

Not with dervish cap or robe is dervish-hood to be attained;
Who of his heart a dervish makes needs not such outer covering.

Put not the blame upon the robe if you have not yet found the Way;
Walk as though the Way you tread – a Path not made for dallying.

Barefoot, with head uncovered, Love toward your Sheykh will guide your steps;
Saints have found their food, have life discovered, though they walked unshod.

Yunus, risen, speaks of Wisdom to all saints along the Way;
He is a comrade with all travellers who journey by this Road.

 53

Not for us the single view: come, let us to the Friend,[33] my heart;
Let us not in longing die; come, let us to the Friend, my heart.

Let us away while life remains, before the form is left behind;
Before the foe has breached the walls; come, let us to the Friend, my heart.

Let us away, not stand apart; let us now for the Friend prepare;
Our place is in the line of Sheykhs; come, let us to the Friend, my heart.

Let us abandon home, and land – though we may grieve for friendship's sake;
To find the meaning of true Love, come, let us to the Friend, my heart.

Be for me a certain guide as now we follow Friendship's Road;
Let us forswear the backward glance; come, let us to the Friend, my heart.

Not resting in the world of form, passing and illusory,
Let us hold fast to Unity; come, let us to the Friend, my heart.

Beyond this world let us progress, soaring above to Friendship's realm;
Let us no longer breathe desire; come, let us to the Friend, my heart.

This our world does not endure; open your eyes, your soul arouse;
Be to me a comforter; come, let us to the Friend, my heart.

Before they tell that we have died, that death has laid his hand on us,
That Azraïl has struck us down; come, let us to the Friend, my heart.

To sainthood let us now attain, seek now God's message to receive;
As comrade Yunus Emre take; come, let us to the Friend, my heart.

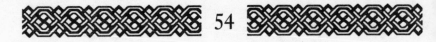 

Once, from the father's loins into the mother's womb there fell the heart;
God it was who so ordained it; into treasure fell that heart.

There, on me, was soul bestowed, into flesh and bone and blood;
Into a span of fleeting days, into movement fell the heart.

I walked alone, secluded, then; not yet God's mercy had I known;
Torn was I from my true home as into this world fell the heart.

First they placed me in a cradle, swaddled tight my hands and feet;
When, bitter taste first on my tongue, into salt[34] then fell the heart.

Each day they unwrap me, twice; with silver coins they deck my brow;
Give my mouth the breast: into the grip of self then fell the heart.

My infancy I set aside, determined in my mind to walk;
But though with puny frame I strove, from this to that hand fell the heart.

When, as a boy, possessed by pride as on me each a kiss bestowed,
My mind companion was to me; and into self-will fell the heart.

I reached the age when joyfully I saw what sprouts on lip and chin;
Then vanity took hold of me and need for love seized on the heart.

I knew the right, preferred the wrong; all I performed in earnest haste;
I thrust away all but desire; deeper in selfhood sank the heart.

At five-and-forty features change, in beard both white and black appear;
On seeing this, into a mood to pluck these out then fell the heart.

Endeavour now brings no success, and arm cannot enforce the will;
Putting aside this doleful state, to graver things then turned the heart.

The son cries: 'Senile, yet won't die;' the daughter: 'Would that he'd lie still.'
Their own state understanding not – into yet others falls the heart.

Grateful are they that death has come, and to the graveyard turn their way,
Repeatedly recall God's name; into 'Thank God' now falls the heart.

44

They bring the water for ablution and the shroud to fold the corpse;
Place upon the bier the body; into death then falls the heart.

If self to effort you have given, the grave is no constraint for you;
Who never for the good has striven – of fiery wine now drinks the heart.

Yunus, know your state; if what your Road must bring you to is this,
While yet your strength abides in you, a means of blessing be, my heart.

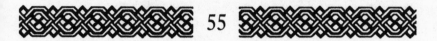 55

Death moves always with us – not for us to know whose turn is come;
It makes a garden of all people, plucks the one it wants from it.

Many the backs it bends in pain, many deprives of all they have;
Tears of grief it makes to flow as Death grinds down with all its power.

From one the loved companion takes away, bereavement's tears it brings;
No mending can the breast so stricken know; Death sickens of the kindly deed.

When vigour is made frailty, Death comes to make its presence known;
It leaves *another* prey, and comes with narrowed eyes *this* one to find.

Where is our moment's Love? Be now obedient, walk in purity;
Poor Yunus tells you: only the monstrous – *that* it is which Death can grind.

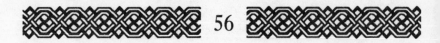 

At dawn I went abroad, by morning's light the place of death I saw;
The graceful forms once flesh, now hidden, in the dark earth laid I saw.

All these both joy and grief once knew, who now lie lonely in each grave;
Where blood had fled the vein and coloured the surrounding shroud I saw.

Headstones tumbled, in disorder strewn, their latter homes in ruin;
How aweful their condition those whom care had now released I saw.

No pasture now on plateau high, nor Winter in the vale below;
Their tongues in silence stilled, their mouths clamped tight for ever now I saw.

Some had lived for merriment, some for grace of word or form,
Some had only sorrow known: their yesterdays today I saw.

Colourless those bright, dark eyes; faded those faces like the moon;
Beneath black earth, the graceful hands which once had gathered flowers I saw.

Convulsed these human forms committed now for ever to the earth;
Those wretched, withered ones who thrust away a mother's love I saw.

Some there are who weep as demons pierce and rive their tortured souls;
And from the flames which had engulfed their tombs the wreathing smoke I
    saw.

Wherever Yunus saw these things he came to give us news of them;
Knowledge once I had, but now confused; and yet these things I truly saw.

You are Mercy, You are Grace; to You O God I stretched my hand;
In none but You have I my cure: to You O God I stretched my hand.

The term was reached, death showed itself, full to the brim the cup of life;
And who shall stay who has not drunk? To You O God I stretched my hand.

My tongue dried up within my mouth, my soul from body wearied now;
As eyelids then begin to droop, to You O God I stretched my hand.

My winding sheet they cut as to Your majesty I turned my gaze;
In wonder what my state should be, to You O God I stretched my hand.

Ready stood my bier when to the four points call to prayer was made;
As for the prayer the people stand, to You O God I stretched my hand.

Then moved they from the rites of death and scattered earth to cover me;
Their duty done they went their way: to You O God I stretched my hand.

Azraīl and Death's twin angels,[35] black of brow, with flaming eyes,
Spoke in turn the word ordained: to You O God I stretched my hand.

They led me to the narrow road, they took me to the hair-breadth bridge;[36]
Trust in myself completely fled, to You O God I stretched my hand.

See, now the time has struck when we cry out in anguish from the heart,
When what is born of mother dies: to You O God I stretched my hand.

Angels, and all creatures, are transported, rapt, in awe they stand;
Now glory yours, awakened ones: to You O God I stretched my hand.

A stranger came I to this land, from which I long now to depart;
The moment come at last when I shall burst the bonds of slavery.

The Friend invites us to His side, His thought is always for our care;
Despite my shame I know that still His blessedness will flow to me.

The substance of the Four Books in my time I often read and taught;
And I have learned that not the pen, not written page, provides our need.

The seven meanings of the Book a single letter[37] manifests;
But save that You give me the Word, I wander, straying from the Road.

Who from that single letter learns remains untrammelled by the world;
Why then do clouds of care envelop me in all my wanderings?

The men the Law gave birth so often seek to bar the Way to me;
Upon Truth's ocean I have been a bird that dives into that sea.

Thence came I where I stand today; *here* was it the One I found;
One with Mansūr, I to the scaffold came – my ashes rise on high.

Bitter and sweet can never be the water rising from one spring;
To mock me is the mode – yet from the conduit still I trickle out!

If yesternights have darkened been, and on my Path is no repose,
If yet I have for guide a saint – why then should I be led astray?

To all the world my guilt is this: that I pronounced the name of Truth;
They flee in fear from treachery – is it for me to rail at that?

Yunus, this is bird-tongue[38] such as Solomon once understood;
I too have sensed the substance which the saints have spoken on this Road.

From the Friend came tidings to me: 'Steadfast stand, and so attain;'
My life to sacrifice I give that, giving it, I may attain.

These two yards of simple cloth, having neither sleeve nor hem,
This shroud should be my robe of honour; wrapped in it may I attain.

When that which takes all life shall come and bid me trust myself to It,
Then may my trust be in the Source of trust, may I through That attain.

My life departed, helpless standing, as I started on the Road;
In knowledge that the friends I knew have too known joy may I attain.

Earth and sky will fill with sound as Death's twin angels come for me;
May I responses give to all they ask that so I might attain.

Many my shameful sins as I untroubled walked in this sweet world;
May I so give account of all I did that yet I might attain.

And still I fear to lose this fragile flesh which I have nourished here;
But let that be with darkest earth co-mingled that I may attain.

Now have I harvested, have gathered in again the fruits of life;
So let these goods be brought to all, cries Yunus, so may I attain.

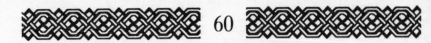 

Here I have no resting place, I came here only to depart;
I came, a wandering pedlar, all my wares on show for those who care.

I came not to dispute, my only occupation is with Love;
I came to fashion hearts here, hearts which are the dwelling of the Friend.

My madness is the drunkenness of Love – all lovers know my state,
I came my dual nature to transfigure, and to merge with One.

I the servant am in Friendship's garden, He the Teacher is;
I came to sing, a nightingale, in joy among my Teacher's flowers.

Souls which here in Friendship dwell, will there be known as they once knew.
I came that, by my Teacher known, I might make offering of my state.

Ask where Yunus may be found: where Friendship is, he too is there;
Come, see, from me His tidings take; it was to see this that I came.

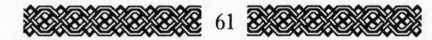 

He Who sent me to this place knows well the work for which I came;
I have no dwelling in this world, it was for service that I came.

Much have I journeyed in this world and touched the hem of many a saint;
I heard the voice which is of Power, and to the pitch of passion came.

I hearts broke down with pungent word, as scorching flame I withered souls;
My secret to all folk made known, as to the world displayed I came.

Idris the tailor I became, and I too weaved the cloth he sewed;
The cry of anguish David's beauteous throat gave forth – this I became.

Moses on Sinai I became; I was the sacrificial ram;
Ali was I with sword in hand as to the battlefield I came.

With visage of that moon in Love, I was as honey spread on lips;
My gaze transfixed by those dark eyes, myself the jet-black brows became.

I was a meadow by the sea; a bucket rising from the well;
Even the prayer that Jesus spoke I was as to my task I came.

I was the moon and filled the world, a cloud and lifted to the sky;
As rain I wept upon the earth; in glory to the sun I came.

To those who trivial talk reject, who eyes have opened on the Road,
To those who, understanding, have made choice, to these in dream I came.

I am the pain-filled cure for hurt; I am the gem in Wisdom hid;
Moses I was on Sinai's mount, from there to realms below I came.

'My Way the place where you must stay,' the voice of Truth comes at the dawn;
On Yunus Emre's tongue the Truth – so, on a tongue, in dream I came.

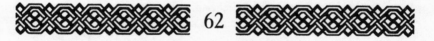 62

To whatsoever place my face is turned I am caught up by Love;
Love it is which stirs my heart, companion with me on the Road.

My Being aches for loveless ones, for them my secret is disclosed;
For when we lovelorn see, the inner self and outer are as one.

This Love, of Mercy's nature is, of all our souls It is the Soul;
And so this struggle with the Evil One is every moment mine.

This my soul is as a bird held fast inside by body's cage;
But when the Friend one day sends word to me I will fly out to Him.

I came, and looked upon the world; I left it this day – or the next;
Here I may not take my ease; here for me is endless toil.

Yunus cries: 'I am a lover, and am faithful to that Love;
This Love display, decay, knows not, such as the fruit of other loves.'

Look not upon me in disdain – I looked upon the Friend and came;
From state and time which have no end, together with the Friend I came.

He it is upon my lips, existence is of Him alone;
My Being only there is found; a stranger to this place I came.

A pedlar I, with goods for sale; my Master and my Friend is Truth;
In Him it was my loss was turned into my gain when here I came.

The seven skies by Love were made, from Love they took their form and shape;
Upon this earth He turned His gaze and rising to my feet I came.

Then saw I the sevenfold Hells, with each and all the eightfold Heavens;
From dross of fear my sin I there refined, as to this place I came.

Adam was I, but did not stay; I failed to wring the neck of self;
I sinned, and ate of that which cast me down from Heaven whence I came.

At the flood Noah I became and for religion's sake I strove;
Who entered not the Ark I flung into the waters when I came.

Falsehood dwells not in my Word: open your eyes, look on my face;
My footsteps still are visible upon that Road by which I came.

In the flesh of Job I was, when torment I brought on my soul;
I called upon my God when I, as flesh, food fed to worms, became.

Zachariah too was I who made his refuge in the tree;
I shed my blood on every side as, head by torment pierced, I came.

With Moses, Sinai's mount I climbed, a thousand-words-and-one I spoke;
The nature of all things created there it was I learned, and came.

Jesus I became – through Power, not womanhood, as they have claimed;
To me came grace from Truth itself; as dead restored to life I came.

I was Girgis on the rack, Mansūr when on the scaffold slain;
As though I were the wool of Hallāj – such the state to which I came.

Upon a night the Truth decreed Mohammed should ascend to Heaven;[39]
The whole of me, from head to foot, I too, in adoration, came.

God, alone, from everlasting was – the Soul in prophets hid;
Yunus's Self in secret lay, and in transfigured form I came.

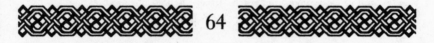 64

The Friend looked on me – since that time I knew the Lord revealed, and came;
All doubt dispelled, to highest in the height in certainty I came.

Take no heed that I be drunk, or say not that you think me mad;
Such drunkenness is of Eternity – I tasted it and came.

From all Eternity I was; to 'Am I not?', 'Yes!' was my cry;[40]
Within that timeless, everlasting sea a current I became.

The heady joy of it I knew, so on my tongue the cry was heard:
'My life, religion, faith, all rendered as thank-offering, I came.'

Love to me became as Jesus, prayers were offered by the saints;
In earthly form, and once again, I perished, yet I rose and came.

Mansūr cries: 'I am the Truth,' and 'Let the flame consume the form;'
Let such to scaffold come – and I my executioner became.

So ask not where is Yunus found: for where the Friend is there is he;
He who sees His gospel gives – in solitude I saw, and came.

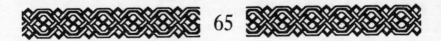 

O beloved ones, O brothers, ask of me where then I was;
In the sea of Love I was engulfed, that ocean swallowed me.

Before all things had yet been born, or angel hosts the skies had filled,
Before creation yet was formed, with Him who formed it I was one.

Where hand of worry could not reach, nor eye behold unhappiness,
Beyond the city of despair, in glory then I had my home.

He who joins with us in this, all turmoil let him lay aside;
More inner than the secret Self, a hidden joy I then had known.

Before I had the Four Books[41] read, and sought to classify, and choose,
I memorized what I was given, and was the minstrel of this Love.

It was my Sultan's licence and command that brought me to this realm;
The dual worlds became my paradise, and I Ridvān became.

He it was stood wait for me, close guarded me in every place;
One with the soul within, I was the taper of the candle flame.

Years without end I was a star, with angels longing in the sky;
When the Omnipotent brought order out of chaos, there was I.

Angels without number shall we stand, rank upon rank above;
Gabriel there I saw when I was in that glorious company.

Ninety thousand are the words which Truth may speak with the Beloved;
But of them one in three will secret be, and in them I was hid.

Before my present form was given, before as Yunus I was known,
He was I, and I was He – with Him who proffered Love, at one.

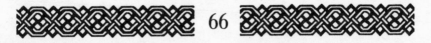 66

He seized my heart, and I know not the wherefore or the why of me;
The Self I am I lost awhile; I search, but Him I cannot find.

Not by *my* will entered I the Path, my speech is not my own;
I crave a sufferer to tell my woe – but such I cannot find.

Yet am I thankful for my hurt though I have mocked it jestingly;
We shall discover, we who grieve, though I myself I might not find.

If they should ask of me who was it took possession of my heart;
How shall I recount what passed when, weeping, I no word can find?

He Who has my heart made captive penetrates the universe;
Wheresoever I may gaze, without Him no place can I find.

He Who gave the cup to Yunus, He it was prayed 'En el Hāk;'[42]
I drank the draught He proffered – now sobriety I cannot find.

 67

Now have I, once again, arrived where I must speak the secret Word;
The single Word by which the earth and sky shall know the sense of awe.

If I so wish life shall come forth; if so I wish flesh shall be formed;
Sinai my heart shall be, Moses my soul, and Love as Solomon.

If what I know as life should challenge me, such living's neck I wring;
But if for me death is decreed, my life I gladly sacrifice.

However Jesus reached his end, may I by like Path reach that Soul;
And from the Way of virtue to the world of Truth may I bring joy.

Who is this Death's angel, Azraīl, who dares to claim my soul?
Within the prison-house of his intent I shall himself restrain.

And Gabriel, who is he who can presume to judge my suffering?
Pinioned beings like him, in their thousands, come beneath my sway.

Those who came this Way before us made of Meaning mystery;
I came to manifest that Meaning born as though a part of me.

Yunus, every Word you speak with Truth's own Being overflows;
Thence I came, that I in lovers' hearts that Being might become.

55

I am both Ka'āba and idolatry – I am the whirling universe;
I am the cloud which rises to the skies and pours its rain on earth.

From loving parents of that dynasty which has its home in hearts,
Who made the Summer, beautified the earth, I learned how I must serve.

I am the flash of furious lightning, writhing and weaving out itself;
I am the poisonous serpent in the black depths of the earth beneath.

Who helped Hamza to scale Mount Kāf,[43] then brought him to bewilderment,
Who put down many from their thrones, the Lord of Wisdom – these am I.

I am the One who, bones and flesh and skin uniting, fashioned us;
I lie in Wisdom's cradle and am suckled with the milk of Power.

To many my commands I gave whose lives passed in prosperity;
The burning coal, the glowing iron, anvil and hammer-wielder – I.

Who freezes earth, snow's fashioner – yet brings to creatures every need;
Know that I to everything am Merciful, Compassionate.

Come then, you who truly love, the right Road you may learn of me;
I am a steadfast signpost to your goal – the City of all Hearts.

An ocean, calling to the waters of this world, Yunus am I:
Self-subsistent, faithful standing, giving form to earth and sky.

 69

I rose together with Mohammed on the Night of the Ascent;[44]
Possessed of nothing, a companion of the Sufi brotherhood.

To these I was a means that they might patience and contentment know;
Though one head from my shirt is seen I am a being fortyfold.[45]

Among that forty, one I wounded sore with keenly cutting blade,
And all the forty, losing blood as one, I caused to understand.

Before our father Adam and our mother Eve had been created
I it was who, destitute, was driven out of Paradise.

I, too, it was who with the prophet Moses Word from God inscribed;
And, with the prophet Jesus, I it is who stands in Heaven above.

With Omar-i Hattāb for justice and for righteousness I strove;
And I was with his son when he his retribution due received.

Ibrahim Edhem looked on his throne and crown – abandoned them,
And entered on the Path; yet I it is who feel that mystery.

Abd ur-Razzāk of the brotherhood companion made of me;
And with Mansūr I too was made to suffer on the scaffold stretched.

Then I took Yunus as my name, made known my secret to the world;
Who will in times to come be on the tongues of men – that one am I.

 70

Since I the Truth discovered in myself, doubt means no more to me;
If I see not the image of the Friend, what are my eyes to me?

Let him approach who prays, who tells the ninety thousand needful things;
Who, praying makes an outward show – see, what is such a friend to me?

On Sinai would I be with Moses and, as eyes effulgent, see;
Become the word the tongue makes sound: what then the trumpet blast to me?

As Moses Sinai I ascend and look on Radiance itself;
Now, here below, save that they see the Friend, what bring my eyes to me?

I made the total of myself, my faith reposing in that Friend;
In reverence rose to Unity – what now is piety to me?

Unlettered was I to that Friend, He called my name 'Illiterate';
Sugar my tongue, my flesh its cane – how stands the speaker then to me?

Yunus the illiterate, with fathers nine and mothers four;
Let me but burn in flame of Love – life's commerce, what is that to me?

I am who is Before and After; for those who live their lives am I;
For those who on the Road have lost direction ready help am I.

To constancy I cleave – to those who strive to find my mystery;
The sightless ones – where shall they see me, when in hearts alone am I?

Who in an instant 'Be!' commanded, formed and looked upon the world,
He Who of His Power furnished it, gave life to Love, am I.

Who laid the level places and thereon the weighty mountains set,
Who wove a cloudy bower above, and dressed the lands below, am I.

I was for lovers both profession and denial of their faith;
In faithlessness, and in Islam – and in the doubting heart am I.

He who harmony creates, who writes in truth the Fourfold Book,
I am: the Koran that He wrote, black lines on pages white, am I.

Who orders this and every place, in Friendship reaching Unity;
A gardener who harmonizes, ornaments the world am I.

Even He Whose order rules the earth, Who makes the day to dawn,
The Master by Whose hand the seas and oceans move in waves, am I.

He Who speech confuses, and Love's cauldron makes to overflow;
Who caused Hamza to scale the mount of Kāf,[46] the venomed snake, am I.

Who utters is not Yunus, but the Self within it is which speaks;
Believing not in final faithlessness, Before and After – I.

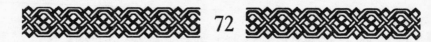 

That secret talisman am I which in these days has been revealed;
The everlasting goal which once I lacked is now for ever mine.

That secret once revealed, all which was dark is now made brilliant;
How many the stages I have passed to reach this body and this life.

I had pronounced the Noble Name in Which this world came into form;
But Adam I took for my name when I into that world had come.

Since they, by looking, see me why do they to others questions put?
Me it is they seek – and I become uncertainty for them.

I have been found in every place, in every atom I was known;
Since everywhere my sound has rung I have to this land, too, been told.

Yunus, what kind of man is this who publishes such mysteries?
Hear then! This music and this flame – each one am I, now come to tongue.

 73

That which I speak is with authority – for I a Firmān hold;
That which I speak shall come to pass; for that my Sultan's Word I hold.

All human ones, all spirits and the fairykind, know my command;
My throne will make the winds to move: the seal of Solomon I hold.

The world to me is sustenance, its peoples and my own are one;
Each moment is for me a judgement which within my heart I hold.

What though men and Satan, each, should err, what though they cause to err?
Whatever is, of good or ill, is mine; for all from Him I hold.

When life like You is there for all, then those who seek the Stream of Life
And still in darkness find themselves, as senseless sorry beasts I hold.

For He is that which makes me live; without His life I am as dead;
Think never that I hold my living higher than that Life I hold.

Religion, faith, for me is He: were I without Him in this world
No idol would I worship, nor the Cross – to no faith would I hold.

Yunus, speak: no doubt can be that He is I, and I am He;
The Friend is true to what I speak – and what the Friend speaks, that I hold.

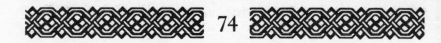 

O Friend, would I were swallowed by Your sea of Love – and so pass on.
Let dual worlds be manifest as I, my time fulfilled, pass on.

I would that Your waters covered me, that I were not Elif, Dal, Mim,[47]
But nightingale in Friendship's bower where blooms are gathered – and pass on.

As nightingale I long to sing, to be a heart in human frame
As, heedless of all other things, Your Road I take and so pass on.

In gratefulness I own that I have seen Your Face, have drunk Your Love;
The city of the 'I' and 'You' I would abandon and pass on.

This is Yunus, wayfarer of Love, bereft of the bereft;
In You is care for all my pain; Your cure I seek, and so pass on.

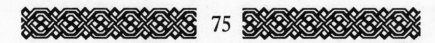 

O Truth, my God – O Truth, my God; none there is like You, my God!
My sinfulness absolve, O You, the Most Compassionate, my God.

To You I make my cry O Lord: what is the balm for this my hurt?
But never spare me, so I ever burn in flames of Love, my God.

Come place me in the centre of that fire that I may be engulfed;
So for Mohammed, Your Beloved, I may become a torch, my God.

Neither in destitute nor rich are You; nor palace nor the lowly home;
But into humble hearts You enter, there make Your abode, my God.

For You are ours, as we Your servants are; many the ills of these,
Yet to Your Heaven direct them; grant they may with Burāk rise, my God.

Learning I have not, neither piety; no strength remains to me,
Save as Your mercy brings to me when You my face make shine, my God.

Bestow on Yunus Your compassion, on Your sinful servants all;
Without Your mercy and forgiveness we are wholly lost, my God.

In this world of dissolution oft-time I am filled with awe;
As oft-time I in joy am lost – and oft-time sorrow seizes me.

Amidst the motions of the world, to angels now I make my pleas;
And now, I am the sun and Heaven's throne, myself celestial.

I measured out my paces, seven and four – when I eighteen surpassed
The nine I left upon the Road that I might be my Lord's command.

The Friend from sorrow brought to us His joy; I offer it to all,
In outward form a man – within I am a soul and a beloved.

Now am I a Mufti, learned in the Law, who sees things clear;
And now, a man deficient; now, a man of prudence in affairs.

Now, with Yunus[48] I discourse within the secret, inner Fish;
Now, to the stars I reach and am, like to Selmān, a thousand souls.

Now, in basest depths below, with Satan I work wickedness;
Now, to the throne of God I rise, and circle with those moving hosts.

Sometimes I hear, yet sometimes I do not – can find no sustenance;
And often, in oblivion, I am both man and animal.

Now, within the compass of men's minds, I am made manifest;
Now, am I of the accursed; now, of the whirling Saturn, lord.

Many are they who monsters are within though clothed in human form,
And often I myself a fox, a wolf, a lion, am become.

How often I have been the separated, and who separates;
And often I am both a man and spirit – and a devil too.

How often on the field of Love I would the steed of self make prance,
And of my head I make a ball for striking on the polo-field.

Sometimes I long to be at one, in one-ness with that very One;
Sometimes I would return, become a droplet – yet the ocean too.

Sometimes I am in hell together with the Pharaoh and Hamān;[49]
Sometimes I am in Paradise, become that beauteous youth Ridvān.

Sometimes I am a fighter, with the Franks upon the battlefield;
Sometimes I am a very Frank – a traitor in oblivion.

Sometimes I am rejected and unknown; sometimes Nemrūd become;
Sometimes I am transformed into Ja'āfer; sometimes a bird in flight.

No-one can meaning find in words which come to me from the Divine;
Hizir has on the Road remained – and I, a circling universe.

So often is a friend made one with me, and I with him am one;
As often in distress and sorrow am I set apart from him.

Earth and air and fire and water[50] I would leave to see His Face,
From chance released, assume the form of formlessness outside this life.

How often do I make the claim 'You-I' or shamelessly, 'I-You';
I long to stand in silent awe released from trickery of tongue.

They ask what means my speech, and yet my Being burns if I speak not;
Then let me speak in pearls, and to the Friend be song of nightingale.

Let me from prison be released to live in dwellings of the free;
But in another prison-house would still be prisoner – and guard.

As to Yunus from Taptūk, so too from Barāk to Saltūk;
Since what was granted to us overflows why should I seek to hide?

That Which is both First and Last – may I be That, and That alone:
Before and After, That abides; and I – might be All save That One?[51]

 77

So it was I knew myself; most surely know I found the Truth.
Only till the finding was the fear – now I from fear am free.

I fall not into slightest doubt; from nobody may fear now come;
For who shall now be cause for fear when I with what I feared am one?

Azraïl approaches not, no Questioners[52] beside my grave;
What questions can they ask of me when I both formulate and ask?

Such time as I became as Him, and will according as He wills,
He came, and filled my heart; I am a shop in which His wares are seen.

Seek the Owner in His shop; He has His substance where He dwells;
To all the people now I am of worth since He is hither come.

The living take us by the hand – how may the lifeless know the saints?
They who take, they also give; of all I am compendium.

Truth the door to Yunus opened, it is that Truth Yunus reveres;
My care is the Enduring State: a slave I was – I am a Lord.

 78

A meagre cup contains the sea yet cannot serve to quench my thirst;
My lamentations know no pause; unceasing tears stream from my eyes.

Come, let us journey to that land, there find the garden, enter in,
Where ever sings the nightingale and never pales the rose's bloom.

The gardens of our land are filled with flowers forever fresh displayed;
In beds attended lovingly my bloom exotic will not fade.

Oft the Beloved to my hand held out the cup that Mansūr drank;
And so the flames blazed higher round me: none there is can know my state.

Upon the Road to the Beloved you burn until you are but ash;
Though in a day I burn a thousand times I will not turn away.

Ferhād I was, as of my soul the pick-axe sharp of Love I forged;
I cleave the hills eternally: my Shirīn seeks no word of me.

Yunus cries: 'My Sultan, Love of You it is has burned my heart;
Give healing to my hurt: so only shall my soul not taste of death.'

O you who call me dervish, what of dervish-hood is there in me?
In Summer uplands of true dervish-hood as Winter are my deeds.

The dervish name I took and clothed myself in all its outer forms;
Yet when I viewed the Way ahead I stood in shame at what I did.

My dervish cap and robe I view with pride, but wrong is all I work;
In every part of me a thousand falsities, and more, are hid.

They look to me for guidance on the Road: I speak, and they believe;
They think me innocent of heart; woe, that such burdens come on me.

If you within me look, there is scarce half a penny's worth to see;
The quarrels and confusions of my outer self whole worlds would fill.

Yunus calls to you: 'O lovers of the Truth, O truly saints;
I now can but commit my state upon this Road to God alone.'

Could it be that there is here another exile such as I,
Whose breast is torn, whose eyes are filled with tears, an exile such as I?

Throughout the realms of Rūm and Shām, and regions of the Upper Lands,[53]
Much have I sought, but never have I found, an exile such as I.

May none be so bereft that they should burn with yearning in such fire;
World's Master mine, may none be ever made an exile such as I.

My tongue pours words, as tears my eyes; my Being aches for sundered hearts;
My star it seems stands separate in the sky – an exile such as I.

How often with this pain I burn; though I for death's release should yearn
Yet in my grave will then be found again an exile such as I.

They say that when an exile dies the death three days remains unknown,
And cold is the water for the washing of an exile such as I.[54]

Yunus Emre mine, O Yunus, pitiful; no balm your wound can find;
From city unto city go your way – an exile such as I.

 81

Heart, you are weary and oppressed by endless journeying;
May God, my God, from every peril keep you ever free.

When humankind oppression knows from other humankind,
Better to go, and never more be seen, than envy find.

Since I was born, by exile from my own have I been driven;
So now my heart's blood trickles, seeps away, from breast so riven.

A field of thorns my country now, the rose-bed exile is;
Better the cup of poison now rather than sugar cane.

Yunus, while yet you travel trustingly towards the Friend,
May God, my God, from every peril keep you ever free.

O my heart, I long had sought to know where you are to be found;
In what is ruined, desolate, laid low – by God, *there* you are known.

The day I to my heart conformed no more of self-regard remained;
God's mercy be, till in whatever place you stand you are possessed.

For but a twinkling you are light – a moment, and you walk bereft
A sign for all to see: for pain you are a captive remedy.

Now in piety you pray, obedient to religion's rules;
A moment, and you are become rebellious, every creed oppose.

We shall pass through, and go beyond, this Love, in torrents overflowing;
Yet there are times, my heart, when you in mosque and in Koran are found.

So Kayseri, Tabrīz and Sivas; Nahjivān, Marāsh and Shiraz,[55]
Even Baghdad, my heart, is near to you – though mad to all the wise.

Yunus, raise yourself in worship, stem the moisture of your eyes;
Whether tomorrow, or today, you are to Truth a sacrifice.

Crazed heart you have again brimmed over; must you, as the waters, rage?
Once more my tears of blood run down: are you to bar the Road to me?

Do what I will I cannot reach my Love, no balm my pain can find;
I am cast out from my true land – and do you seek to hold me here?

I lost my comrade on the Road, since when I have no solace found;
My heart's blood! Must you well within me till, as tears, you pour from me?

Along your Road I am as dust – and yet more you demand of me:
Are you the mountain which, in stony challenge, stands athwart my Way?

You snow-topped mountain hard across my Path like to a highwayman;
Torn as I am from my true Love, would you now close the Road to me?

You clouds that gather round the crags of these same snowy mountain peaks,
Is it for me, your tresses flowing, that you bear unbroken tears?

Yunus is beside himself; my destination hid from me;
The meaning he cannot divine when Yunus glimpsed You in a dream.

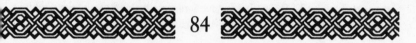 84

If that Friend should not come to us, let us return to find the Friend;
Though stricken sore with suffering, to see the Friend's Face is my end.

His Love has taken hold of this poor piece of earth that is my all;
Who is there seeks for goods within a marketplace without a stall?

But should a stall be set in the bazaar, the Friend will enter there;
My heart knows I have wrongly wrought, so to the Friend my plea I bear.

My heart tells me the Friend is mine, my eyes tell me the Friend is mine;
My heart bids me be patient: still I long for tidings of my Friend.

Unfaltering look full upon a soul on which the Truth has gazed;
For us it is not to deride the one whom Truth has looked upon.

Taptūk yet speaks to Yunus: 'Should this love of yours to Truth attain,
*This* is sublimity.' My journey then shall not have been in vain.

Fill me so with awe that I may burn within the flame of Love,
That whatsoever thing I look upon I find You always there.

Since when my Sultan called to me my soul set out upon the Way;
Since I am here but as a guest, how should I then in dalliance stay?

That which is called the sevenfold hell is nothing to my suffering;
Your Love has me despoiled: how shall I have the strength to suffer it?

Since when my soul has smelled Your fragrance I have cast away the world;
I know not where You are: show me the place where those who seek may find.

In every instant tidings come of You, yet never are You seen;
Draw back the veil that hides Your face from me that I may meet Your gaze.

My soul tempestuous as the seas, my body tosses like a shell;
Then let me sink, be swallowed, in the waters of the double sea.

If I should cross the seven seas and drink the rivers seventy
My thirst will be unquenched – for only Friendship's draught can satisfy.

The lovers told me of four ways of faith: through seven my soul has swum;
Say not how many witnesses have testified that I am mad.

If they should yearn for eightfold heaven let seventy thousand houris come;
But shall it be that these entice my heart, and such deceive my soul?

Whose reading is in books of knowledge, these may never taste of Love;
Mansūr I am – let me but live on lips of men, though slain today.

This Word of Yunus is a cry to fill the souls of all;
The negative but sightless stay before whatever I display.

I am that orphaned pearl which depths of ocean never yet have seen;
A drop I am that to the ocean is as much an ocean too.

Come, see the waves of wonder which conceal the seas of mystery;
Though they are endless, yet these waters wide within a drop are hid.

Mansūr did not dispel the Unity when he cried: 'En el Hāk;'
Through Friendship's love-lock on Love's scaffold here in nakedness I hang.

In this world of multitudes Joseph are you, and Jacob I;
And yet no Joseph is, nor yet Ken'ān, in the Real world of Unity.

In that world Mejnūn the lover never called on Leyla's name;
But I myself was Leyla – and Mejnūn I was, her worshipper.

Before Ye, Nūn and Sin[56] arrived, or soul in body's mould was poured,
I came here drunk with Love's delight; could I with that same taste depart!

This body burdensome becomes since now it bears Yunus's name;
If you should seek to know me – to the Sultan I a sultan am.

From nation, faith, He banished me Who made a captive of my soul;
The one who hears His voice no more has heart or soul to call his own.

Those who do not sense my state upbraid me: 'He has faith forsworn;'
With what shall faith give nourishment to one who has no heart, no soul?

In form I had conceived my Being to be one with heart and soul;
Of both He left me destitute, that One Who on me Love bestowed.

Love's sentinel has never held forbidden from me anything;
Not in Islam, not in creeds, is faith – or faithlessness – recalled.

The rule imperative will not be found where life in Love is lived;
A tongue which no response receives – who is it can this language know?

He made the hand to rest from toil, caused care to come to those in pain;
In Friendship's marketplace we have no memory of loss – or gain.

He drove me from my outward self, cancelled the balance sheet of life;
They know no more of fear or want who put aside all 'good' and 'ill'.

Ask not for news of Yunus, where he is – where Friendship dwells is he;
He sets at naught a hundred thousand gems who dives into Love's sea.

Today, discourse in Love is ours – who 'ours' confesses, let him come.
The one who lovingly can drink Love's poison potion, let him come.

Into 'contentment''s cloak the head of fearful 'caution' I withdrew;
I shaped the shirt of 'shiftlessness' – if wise would wear these let them come.

Within the marketplace of Love I raised my voice and cried my heart;
As though a muezzin, I call: 'Who is at one with me may come.'

This ocean covers jewels numberless which hand has never held;
Its waters, full of mercy, overflow; who would be clean may come.

Hear my words my friends: in yesterdays it was I made today,[57]
And then I lost myself; who would the true Path travel, let him come.

Yunus the wretched saw it so; took to his hand a book of verse
Such as the learned have not read: who hears its Meaning, let him come.

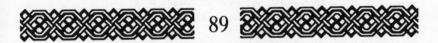

## 89

You chant: 'With Him no partner is,'[58] and yet a partnership you claim;
Who gave command to you to make Duality of what is One?

Faith and creed can only spring from righteousness and Truth, naught else;
From what is partial, incomplete, can you religion fabricate?

Since it was Heaven which sent us the Koran, God in the Word partook;
From God His gospel give then – chirp not always bird-like of the Book.

Tome on tome of commentary you read – much grief you draw from such;
Tartar-like you claim that neither want nor fear is found in you.

Con not the written page – absorb: true Being is to know your Self;[59]
If to yourself you are unknown, with brutishness you are but one.

The sum of science is no more than precept from another's mind;
When you no precept can perceive you can but blindly cast a stone.

The Meaning of the Fourfold Book in Mustafa was codified;
You have forgotten this it seems when peddling your commentaries.

Falsely you bow in prayer; shameful in much, of blessing near bereft;
Give ear with care, see where your words can lead – to very hell itself.

You make pronouncement to the people, you yourself hold not to it;
Full of words – but lacking works – in sloughs of sinfulness you sink.

In doctrines you expound no dawn will rise on we poor mendicants;
Yet come with open heart, and you will see you are no more than we.

If you make claim that we have erred from what has been prescribed by Law,
Success will not attend your case: your care, master, leads you astray.

Yunus the wretched, from within Love's universe, proclaims this Word:
Speak not save what within is known – the added word is but your own.

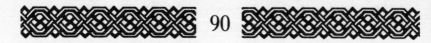 

We are lovers; what have we to tell that is more sweet than Love?
It is to those who hear that I would speak of Love, with each discourse.

This Love may not be circumscribed, by no analogy is bound;
Not in this world nor the world to come Love's substitute is found.

It is unjust to prate of Love to those who Love have never known;
To one who is a lover in all Truth I may unveil my all.

Take heed, take heed! Be sure that you guard well that which is told of Love;
In place unworthy of the trust speak not the mystery of It.

All traffickers in gems know well that in their trade the rule is this:
Make not your jewels a display for those who cannot know their worth.

Who, in the pre-Creation feast of friends the Face of Friendship saw,
His is the Lover's soul: of him you may seek tidings of His Love.

While yet nor earth nor sky had been created Love in Being *was*;
For Love eternal is – whatever *is* of you was born of Love.

All that Yunus comprehends is of a breast with Love made full;
His hurt he could not hide – compelled, Love's secret he reveals to all.

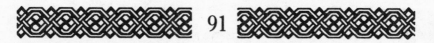 91

I found the Soul of every soul; my own soul freely I give up;
Of gain and loss I know no more – such commerce freely I give up.

I have transcended 'I'; the veil before my eyes is drawn away;
Now, in the presence of the Friend, all doubt I willingly give up.

My Self has sloughed off self, all self's possessions to the Friend returned;
Giver and taker is the Friend: my speech I willingly give up.

Attachment brought me only woe; swiftly I flew to seek the Friend;
I fell into Love's poetry – my own I willingly give up.

I wearied of Duality; in Unity's abode refreshed,
The wine of hurt and grief I drank: my cure I willingly give up.

When Being set out on the Road the Friend came out to welcome us;
The broken heart was bathed in light; my world I willingly give up.

From endless forethought freed, now Summer's heat and Winter's cold but pall;
I have the chief of gardens found – my own I willingly give up.

Yunus, you thought you pleasure knew as once you honey-sugar sipped;
Since I the hive of hives have found, my own I willingly give up.

 92

My eyes are but to see You with, my hands to stretch, reach out, to You;
Today my soul starts on the Road to find You with the morrow's dawn.

Today my soul sets out in trust that You will give tomorrow's prize;
Offer not Your Heaven to me – my eyes are not upon the skies.

Heaven is no fit place for me; my heart I do not set on it;
I make no tearful supplication for the garden of a *sect*.

Heaven, that Heaven which is held out to us, has often led astray;
I do not pine for mansions, or to clasp sweet houris in my arms.

Here You have abundant houris given to us, without sin;
There is my longing elsewhere fixed: in You I would my refuge find.

Give Heaven to those devout in faith; for me – I need but You alone;
Not for pavilions fair, for shady arbours – but for You – I long.

Yunus for You in longing stands; Your longing show to him in turn;
Unless in cruelty You deal, Your justice give that he might come.

Mohammed's soul was formed by God of radiant light celestial;
Upon the world He poured abundant mercy in Mohammed's name.

In Love He made him as a friend, watched over him in loving care;
And to Mohammed He entrusted care of those who turn to Him.

Mohammed is a sea which all the world embraces in its flood;
The saints the water-fowl who congregate about Mohammed's lake.

Not to this world's goods he held, nor any faith reposed in them;
No tailor sewed a seam in cloth that served to fold Mohammed's frame.

God's lion, Ali, has his place upon Mohammed's right-hand side;
And on Mohammed's left the brothers Hasan and Huseyn stand.

In all their thousands every year the pilgrims[60] take the holy vow;
They set out on the journey which will take them to Mohammed's light.

Yunus, the old in years, is full of Love – yet lacking, pitiful;
He only hunger knows who from Mohammed's table does not taste.

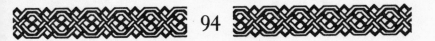 

If I bring news of Love which saints have known, will you give ear to me?
And would you be prepared to make your journey on this Road with me?

Even the entrance to the Way to that far land is suffering;
Would you to others sweetness give, and take the poisoned cup yourself?

That country vineyards has, though bitter are the fruits they bring;
Can you taste of the wine no beaker can contain, which comes of them?

That firmament no morrow knows, no birth and death of sun and moon;
Can you, abandoning all plans, your mind release from numbers' bonds?

Surrendering all 'you-ness', 'I-ness', on the Road to 'nothing-hood',
Can you, in drinking of Love's cup, your very Being, self, forsake?

Their substance comes to Adam's breed of earth and water, fire and air;
Then tell me, Yunus, in but earth and water – is your Being *there*?

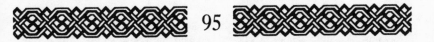 

Take heed that you apportion not your heart to this world's goods one day;
Who so his heart bestows will wake to find that he has dreamed, one day.

This world a monster is, which Adam's sons and daughters can devour;
It may become our turn to fall into its hungry maw, one day.

Do you not see the earth reclining with the wealthy in its clasp?
We too, like them, could find ourselves in that same fond embrace, one day.

A bird which has its nest where hawk or falcon may swoop down on it –
Where in that moment shall it flee? It will go to its end, one day.

Yunus, helpless and forlorn, to sainthood's hem stretch out your hand,
Until you are within Truth's flooding waters swallowed up – one day.

Who would with all their heart take to the dervish Road, let them draw near;
Who from their hearts have driven all that is not Truth, let them draw near.

That which goes by name of dervish-hood is substance infinite;
Who would partake of it, whatever be their state, let them draw near.

As to the sky his prayer ascends the dervish knows both ebb and flow;
I would to all speak right: who does not heed his life, let him draw near.

Dervish-hood is but a morsel – yet more vast than earth and sky;
Who would this noble morsel swallow and absorb, let him draw near.

The dervish eye is ever open, day and night it never sleeps;
God is my witness to this Word: if, looking not, you see – draw near.

That which the dervish feels as Truth – that Truth is all his lesson here,
Though never lip nor tongue should move; if you would hear that Word – draw
      near.

The dervish arm is long, it blinds the eyes of those who would deny;
Those who would straightly come, who err not east nor west, let them draw near.

The dervishes are friends to Truth, their souls are but Truth's drunkenness;
They burn as candle flames of Love: those who are moths, let them draw near.

See then Yunus, destitute, whom dervish-hood has brought to this;
Of self is his complaint – who wish to die to self, let them draw near.

O you who give to me the Sufi name – who say that I am good;
To wear the cap and robe – is this alone the state of Sufihood?

I placed the cap upon my head, and so a Sufi I appear;
An empty hive I am within – my robe for outward show I wear.

Recitation on my lips, yet still my heart plans treachery;
Is this how they recite the name of Truth who to Him true Love bear?

My tongue holds not its proper place but falsehood shows by argument;
My eyes have lost sight of Your Road; Your word I keep not which ears hear.

Yunus knows with certitude the false stay ever on the Road;
But, whether of false or true, we all, one day, will find what we hold dear.

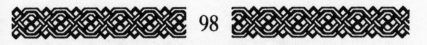 98

O saintly one, on you I call: rise early for the latter prayer;
Unless you should be wholly dead, rise early for the latter prayer.

Listen to the muezzin, he calls to you the name of God;
Demolish not religion's base – rise early for the latter prayer.

The birds soar to the heights above; the trees their rosary recite;
Brothers, sisters, take God's grace – rise early for the latter prayer.

Prostrate yourself, His praise recite, lift up your hands in thankfulness;
In knowledge of your certain death rise early for the latter prayer.

Perform the prayer that is a prop, a pillar of the world to be;
May heavenly light shine on your grave; rise early for the latter prayer.

Prostrate yourself with the imam; doubt never as you rest in sleep
That you will yet depart in faith; rise early for the latter prayer.

From each of us this life departs, this flesh we all shall leave behind;
Yunus the dervish you, too, still rise early for the latter prayer.

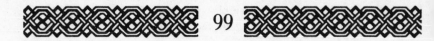
This world in which we live – how shall I liken it but to a mill;
And heedlessness its grindstone is which will this people make as flour.

A mill indeed this world, and God it is to Whose command it moves;
By Azrail's hand He turns the stone with which He grinds the flour so fine.

The universe, as runnel, takes the flour; God's Being turns the wheels;
Give thanks to Him Who puts in motion such machinery as this.

By *Him* those whirling wheels revolve; beyond the runnel take your place;
Your care it is contaminates His grain – forethought it is destroys.

Found not a dervish home, O Yunus, thinking that more ears will hear;
Many there are who know – and know far better than you know yourself.

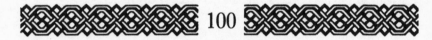
Once more Spring's gentle breezes blowing bring to us its special joy;
It is Your bounteous fullness makes an end to Winter's cold again.

Once more incomparable mercy, merry-making, music time;
Once more the Summer is new born, and happiness comes fresh again.

Once more is nature robed in garments new with treasure newly given;
New life once more on all bestowed, the trees and shrubs bedecked again.

All things which grow, and had been dead, rise up and are reborn once more;
A sign for those who God deny: new generation comes again.

Once more the desert is made green, and swiftly bubbling brooks are heard;
The land in friendship lives as to all worlds the gift is given again.

Once more earth's face is fair with ornament, colours and hues combine;
The nightingale sings to the rose as life breaks from the bud again.

It is not Summer, Winter, that I sing – it is the Lover's work;
To what He had condemned the Sultan wills to grant life once again.

Yunus once more is held in trance, his honour and his name made naught
As, from that noble cup which lovers know, he takes a sip again.

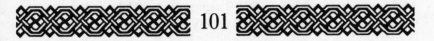 101

Those who dervish-hood would have bestowed on them,
Their hearts in purity should hold, as silver, shining.

Their breath shall be the scent of ambergris and musk;
So cities, provinces, shall flower from their shoots.

Their foliage shall bring to every hurt its cure;
And, in their shade, for all a blessing shall be found.

The tears that flow from lovers' eyes become a lake,
And from its bed is born that reed which gives the flute.[61]

Each minstrel is a nightingale in Friendship's bower –
And Yunus is, amongst them, as a francolin!

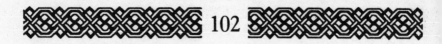 

If both the worlds a prison are, they may for me a garden be;
No sadness, no more sorrow, when the Friend His favour shows to me.

Would that I were Friendship's slave; then would I be both rose in bloom
And sweetly singing nightingale – my home the rose-garden of joy.

My eyes have seen the Lover's face, though to the saints I am as dust;
Yet those who comprehend may find my words as sweet as sugar cane.

They who argument discard, who fly in faith to Truth alone,
Who deeply drink the wine of Love – these find in drunkenness delight.

As yet the dual worlds appear to me as though my prison house;
The purest of the pure are those who know, and are known, in Your Love.

Truly the hypocrite is blind – the morrow will bring shame to him;
The bitter word the people speak to me shall be as sugar, sweet.

Unceasingly in gratitude I bow in prayer before my God;
My 'I-ness' to the Friend I leave – let others from this dispute raise.

Open your eyes while you are here; your inwardness speak openly;
May these your words, O Yunus, to all worlds be told as songs of praise.

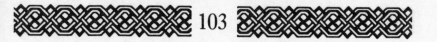 

Who once Your face has seen, for all his life holds You in memory;
You are a rosary for him which keeps him from all other faiths.

If he should catch but glimpse of You, who holds himself in piety,
To *Your* mihrāb he then would turn, and would forget his rosary.

If one there be whose mouth tastes sweetness, then finds You in what he sees,
The sugared mouthful swiftly he forgets before he swallows it.

If they should ask to know the cost to me that I could love You so,
My answer to them is: 'The worth of both the worlds would not suffice.'

Were the two worlds brimful of beds of flowers in blossom without cease,
Basil and rose could not compare with that sweet fragrance which is You.

Should houris in adornment from the eightfold Heaven descend to us,
Grant that my heart accept no other Love save only Love of You.

The scent of rose and basil is to me like lover and beloved;
Grant that the vision of the loved one never fade from lover's eyes.

When Israfil the trumpet sounds and all creation rises up,
Grant that my ears may nothing hear save only praises of Your name.

Should Venus from the sky descend, and stroke her harp to glorious sound,
Be *You* my sole delights – and never may my eyes lose sight of You.

How, of a world and life which know You not, may any make a home?
Better by far than both the worlds are You – of this let no one doubt.

Since ever Yunus loved You, life and beauty are to him as one;
His life each moment new created – age may never wear it out.

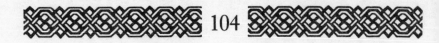 

We drank of that sweet cordial which flows from Truth, praise be to God;
We have passed over, and beyond, the seas of power, praise be to God.

In safety and in joy we have surmounted all that lay ahead –
Through vineyards, oaken groves and towering mountain peaks, praise be to God.

Parched we were and found refreshment; from the lowly we were raised;
Wings we were granted, birds became, and rose in flight, praise be to God.

And in those lands to which we came, bearing in our hearts delight,
We spread abroad to all the message of Taptūk, praise be to God.

Let us now live in reconciliation who had once been foes;
Our horses saddled stand – we take the Road again, praise be to God.

We wintered in the land of Rūm, both well and ill we laboured there;
Then came the Spring and to our lands we turned again, praise be to God.

We were a spring, our waters welled; we rose and spilled, became a stream;
We flooded, flowed into the standing sea beyond, praise be to God.

We were a servant in the hearth and doorway of Taptūk's abode;
Poor Yunus, then raw flesh, has now been made true food, praise be to God.

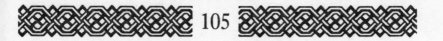 

Let me recount the nature of my life, tell it in detail fine;
Singly or in concourse, near or far – each one I would should know.

Rebellious, loyal, great or small – the Friend as servants knows them all;
And who may see the Sovereign's face unless the servant shows the way?

The Road that leads us to the Friend is that which passes through the heart;
Barren my deeds till I a heart had entered, naught could I fulfill.

Those who journey to the Friend, in travelling forget themselves;
In whatsoever place I am, know that the Friend has led me there.

Where 'you' and 'I' are to be found, there all are sundered, separate;
For how may he who grasps Duality with Unity unite?

Had I not, with the Friend, learned what for all things is the proper end,
My life, till now, in love of insubstantial things had passed away.

Long would the story be in whole; how shall I bring it to an end?
Which from all the list of my shortcomings have I means to tell?

This rule I give: to kiss the feet of all the nations of the earth;
For there, in every nation, may you find the loved one whom you seek.

If he were truly lover Yunus would today have found his Love;
But how shall Love make Its abode relying on tomorrow's Word?

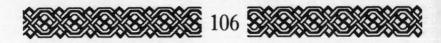 

Tell me, dulcimer and zither, what is your reality?
To you I question put, and wait to hear you speak the Truth to me.

'Of wood' they said 'they fashion us, and of the entrails of a sheep;
Yet hear the guidance that we give – ignore, heed not, the outward shape.

They say we are by Law forbidden: but *we* share not in thievery!
So, what if we of sheeps' insides are made? By this are we unclean?

They make a mockery of what we are, and that we call to Love;
Our name indeed by Love was given – *we* do not lead mankind astray.

In happiness we came into this world, and spread through it our joy;
In ordered blessings are we found, and in a dream we have our place.

They flayed a tree to make us, true; and with a gut completed us;
But after, in the sea of Love we plunged: this is no empty claim.

It is in ecstasy and music that we discourse with our Lord;
Then Wisdom is in Meaning swallowed up – when we with angels live.

Think upon the angels – learn from them what is your true desire;
Since day and night, in everything you do they have their place by you.

Among those angels are the Holy Ones who every life record,
Who, every season of the year, rest not their pens, nor ever err.

Their place is by each shoulder – one upon the right, one on the left;
The one writes down the blessed deed performed, the one records the ill.

The ink they use is of each self which they transcribe; nor it, nor paper
Ever is consumed, nor pen wears out, in their unceasing task.

Know, that in the tavern and the idol-house they go with you
Though they are hid, and you, in heedlessness, have put them from your mind.'

Yunus, glorify the only God, and in your heart give praise;
Not other are this zither and this dulcimer than Wisdom's ways.

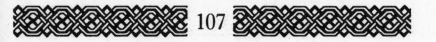 

That which long I sought I found was manifest within my soul;
For what my Being searched for outwardly was there, in flesh, within.

That which, self-subsistent, never errs, without Which not one lives,
Which step by step Its measure takes within the very soul itself.

What binds this talisman of power – is told by every tongue on earth –
What all the lands and sky cannot contain – has entered in this frame.

Though one should be a thief, thieves too within themselves give It abode –
Become the guardians of the law inside the prison of themselves.

'Hold him,' It cries, while ever yet the thief, unchecked, pursues his way;
A wondrous thief – no other than the one who makes the hue and cry!

This power It is Which gives the rule when death is meted out to us;
And It is death itself become within the execution place.

It balances the sword of power and on the nape of self takes aim –
Strikes – and makes the head of self to roll, its hands by blood besmeared.

Who *hears* the fame of the Koran, laments that *others* are unsound;
But only he who reads *himself* in the Koran can read it true.

That It is Who builds pavilions, palaces and hospices;
And often, darkly masked, lies in a cellar hidden deep below.

From head to foot It is the Truth alone Which holds you, keeps you safe;
Nothing there is abiding save that Truth – this must you never doubt.

If you are one, then come to Unity, Duality forsake,
That you may find the whole Reality in faith which is unfeigned.

So hear, and hear – then hear again the tongue of Wisdom speaking true;
Those words of Wisdom which in *knowing* the Koran will come to you.

The City of the Heart I entered, in Its depths immersed, thought-free
In wondering love I gazed – and there it was, in Life, I found the trace.

I tracked that trace I found and, as I travelled, marked on either side
Such things of marvel that may never else be seen upon this earth.

Yunus, they who understand will know the Meaning in your words;
And may they speak those words according to the times in which they live.

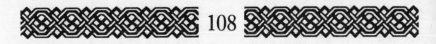

## 108

You who are mad with Love, why stand you so in such diffused distress?
That which has made you so is in yourself, within your very self.

That Truth, Which consubsists with this world and the next, fills earth and sky;
No eye there is can ever see nor It nor what It purposes.

In taverns I have sat, yet never saw a place where It is not;
And even in the public baths with It I often remonstrate.

Who makes material form his aim on earth will find in it his foe;
For him, not this world nor the next is found in profit or in loss.

'Flee,' Its voice to many comes; to others, 'Stay' is Its command;
And with the one in flight It flees, and stays with him who holds his ground.

The Truth it is Which, in affliction, binds us fast as slaves to It;
Yet still within the prison house It stretches out Its hand in help.

'Poor Yunus, what is it,' they cry to me, 'which sends your wits awry?'
They seek in vain intelligence of those who hear this Mystery.

## 109

A Moon I saw this night more lofty than the Zodiac entire;
My heart, my very soul, It so entranced I was as one possessed.

With radiance from that Moon it is enlightenment comes to this world;
That noble Teacher with Its beam a lantern lit within my heart.

Its brightness is Mohammed's light, the secret of the Friend of God;
Such brilliance as, to human minds, a casement were flung wide in Heaven.

The eye of the accuser sees no more when we are one with It;
Whose need it is may yet go hundred times on noble pilgrimage.[62]

The Lover's words it is make tears, that are as blood, flow from our eyes;
When nightingales together sing the time of songless birds is passed.

What make they of a withered tree? Just such a withered tree is he
Who never has a lover been: they cast it in the fire at last.

He who praises Yunus, let him praise – and he who curses, curse;
In Love we started on the Road: when night comes let us then sleep fast.

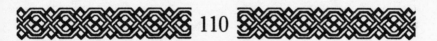 **110**

A lover I became in joining with the saints;
The Truth I found when I the face of sainthood saw.

I came to Man-hood: there I found my heart's desire
Which I, in asking outwardly, could never find.

Then, in whatever place I looked, a saint I saw
Whose heart was captive made by my humility.

What is to every soul by Truth so freely given
May yet not come to us by pilgrimage alone.

The Ka'āba, know, is but the threshhold of yourself;
I came not to it in my *outward* journeying.

Those seeing me had counted me as nothing worth
Who now, at sight of me, with finger point me out.

A lake I was; when saints their gaze bestowed on me,
Filled with their fourfold rivers I became a sea.

A voice came: 'Yunus' – struck by awe I could not move –
My eyes I opened when my ears were tuned to Love.

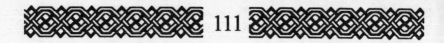 

We hold once more within our hands the warrant true which Meaning gives;
The Sultan of the world has on our tongue bestowed the Word of Truth.

The Truth it is which speaks the Word that brings astonishment on all;
But those who have not understanding cannot share this state of ours.

Our secret they do not partake, are not companions on the Road;
Who is not worthy of that state may not our ecstasy endure.

In ecstasy be one with us, companion in our journeying;
What doubts you have, make known – and bow to that Nobility we see.

This is secret treasure, hid – what do Sufis look to find?
Upon our lake, contentedly, sport water-fowl of *every* kind.

Not *this* world but the visage of Eternity we worship here;
The latter world we recognize – in *these* lands we live gratefully.

Become the ocean, Yunus, plunge into the seas of heavenly light;
Receive, hold to, the Word of Truth: be of the substance of the Right.

In whomsoever sainthood lives let him come in humility;
If he from heights above looks down – his ladder will be pulled away!

What is within will to the surface seep for all the world to see:
The heart which travels full of pride will ever take the errant way.

A greybeard venerable, who lacks all understanding of his state,
Who breaks another's heart – let him not spend his strength on pilgrimage.

The heart is God's own throne, and God has every human heart in care;
Unhappy in both worlds is he who makes destruction of a heart.

Deaf to all, no word he hears; night from day cannot discern –
The negative sees not – no matter though the world is bathed in light.

Excess of words the brute oppresses; so their dearth weighs down the saints;
If you the inner jewel know, this Word will satisfy your need.

What you for self would wish to see wish not for others differently:
For this the Meaning is entire of the Four Books – if such there be.

You know that those who came before have gone, returned to their own land,
And those who sensed the Meaning – these were they who drank the wine of Love.

Grant that Yunus never errs, nor stands in loftiness of pride;
If Whom he loves the Lover is, let him not see the graveyard bridge.[63]

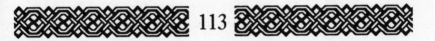 113

Let me speak a Word to you – hear it if you have a soul:
Begrudge not, be not covetous, if you have made your mind to Love.

This Truth we learned of Meaning: Love prefer, even to kith and kin;
Much sweeter is it – if that Love be honest – even than a son.

If you should falseness see in it abandon all, and save yourself;
This is the Wisdom of experience, if you have ears to hear.

The one you love, hold him in reverence as though he were yourself;
Your very body give for food, should you occasion see for it.

To eat another's bread, and trample on his salt is base ingratitude;
Deny not bread to anyone when they have paid to salt the due.

Goodness is the saint's beloved; dying, his Love in Heaven finds;
Whatever is alive in you will be recalled when you are gone.

That wretched Yunus is a madman every word he speaks makes clear;
Beloved ones, reproach him not whatever fault there is in him.

How shall you find the Truth if you be not prepared that Truth to serve;
If you do not prostrate yourself upon the threshold of the saints?

The vineyard that is left untended will with briar become entwined;
What shall you have to say unless you first within the fire be fired?

But in the desert, lonely place what will you find to light the flame,
Where there is nowhere to be seen kindling or tinder for a spark?

Remain not where no people are; let not the flame of Love die down;
Unless the hearth itself is reached how will the blaze by you be found?

The sun of Truth yet rises from the Zodiac of Unity;
Its beam will never shine on Yunus till he rends the veil of Shame.

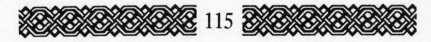 

Until I tasted of the wine of Love I nothing had of sense;
My Being I knew not until I found the nature of true Man.

How can he to that stage attain who on himself in whole relies?
Whose hand the skirt of sainthood has not touched will never reach to God.

If of religion you have need, and faith, then in this world do good;
The uncompleted labour of *this* world will not be finished *there*.

As nightingale is lover to the rose, so Truth loves those who serve;
The tongue can speak no Word of Truth until in hearts of fire refined.

This secret in my heart breaks out in speech, my pain will not be hid;
A lover can no word endure which brings no taste of Love to him.

Poor Yunus, only those who truly lovers are may hear his Word;
Bird-tongue[64] is his – no comfort can he know unless it be with song.

If I without You enter on the Road I have no strength to walk;
For You are all the power my body holds to take me on my Way.

My heart, my soul, my mind, my sense, subsist in me through You alone;
Our need is Love, the pinion of the soul, to soar up to the Friend.

Who traitor is to his true Self will, as a hawk, rend his Beloved;
Will dive on that which swims upon the pool, the gentle water-fowl.

The Lord of Power has given to lovers Hamza's strength a thousandfold,
Who mountains moved to open up the Way that takes them to the Friend.

A hundred thousand Ferhāds mountains yet dig up with their own hands,
And rocks still rive to scour a channel for the Stream of Life to flow.

The fountain of that Stream of Life is wheresoever lovers meet;
Whose cup is filled with that pure water quenches with it every thirst.

The seven satanic streams will be dried up by grief of those who love,
Whose wish it is to bathe the eightfold Heaven in light celestial.

But may I give the name of 'lover' to the one who longs for Heaven?
For Heaven itself is but a trap in which the faithfuls' souls are snared.

The lover will be humble, self-surrendered, on the Road to Truth;
Yet holds himself against the world – he may not flee the broken heart.

You know that many came before you and have, heedless, gone again;
But it is not the ones who drink the wine of Love who pass that way.

Yunus's soul is not beguiled by thoughts of Heaven or of Hell;
Upon the Path he travels to the Friend – true sunset of the soul.

I am without a place in *this*, the passing world – for my abode is *there*;
As King, my crown and throne, my robe, my heavenly steed[65] they all are there.

Who knows what aerial thing I am, each moment to that Face drawn up;
My cup I now have drained, but was from everlasting drunken there.

I came to be a nightingale, to be a song on every tongue;
I am a deer become, my musk to sell – but my true pasture's there.

I stood upon the globe of Atlas, joined with the planets in their dance;
Though here my eyes but darkly see, I saw Mohammed's radiance there.

As Job I knew oppression too, as Girgis died a thousand deaths;
Alone I came into this world, and all of worth to me is there.

Mansūr, I to the scaffold came; as Joseph, sold to slavery;
To hunt I came here in a lion's form but know my lair is there.

I overflow in madness, cannot find my way to common folk;
But though this Word I do not hear, in trance I know my ear is there.

The secret Word speak not: in fire, unhurt, the salamander lies;
By day and night he burns unquenched; so too my own light I find there.

Since Yunus was caught up in these imaginings the world is fled;
And yet, by God, what savour with my senses have I tasted there!

If you instruction and example need, come, look upon these graves;
Come, melt, pour out your overflowing feelings as you gaze on them.

Much had they of this world's goods, but what is their condition now?
A single shirt they had to wear at last – and that a sleeveless one!

Possessed of all – yet palace and pavilion could not satisfy;
Where are they now? Within a cell they dwell, topped by a cap of stone.

No home have they to rest in now; no more ascetic piety
Nor feudal greatness will they find, now that their age is passed away.

Where are they who once so sweetly sang, whose faces shone with joy?
So lost are they that what was written on their stones may not be read.

These once were Beys and Lords of power, with sentries standing at their gates;
Come now, and see – you may no longer tell which Lord is, which is slave.

To them all gates have now been closed, of blessing are they all bereft;
Light they can no longer see – and all their days are yesterday.

One day, O Yunus, you will say of self what now you say of these;
For what to them He brought at last, the same fate He will bring to you.

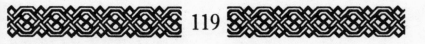 119

My days in emptiness I spent; what may I make of you my life?
By you I found no place – O God; what may I make of you my life?

I came and, learning nothing, went; weeping my sorrow could not quench;
Yet sought not severance from you; what may I make of you my life?

When good and ill is written and the string of life is shortening,
When what is form begins to fade, what may I make of you my life?

Once you depart you come not back – you will not find me if you come;
Myself is all my treasure now; what may I make of you my life?

Was it not in you I trusted, though I harshly dealt with you?
What now remains is all I gained; what may I make of you my life?

Wretched Yunus, you shall go; the wondrous journey you shall take;
But still in longing will you linger; what may I make of you my life?

It swiftly passed, this life of mine, as that sweet breeze which faintly blows;
Truly it comes to me as though it were the twinkling of an eye.

The Truth is witness to my word: the soul dwells as the body's guest;
The day will be when it must go – like to a caged bird when released.

Poor son of Man who has been likened to a sower in the field;
And some spring up, some wither where they lie – like to the very seed.

My Being flames, I burn within, for what I know not in this world,
Like him, who in his prime, had for the dead brought Heaven's harvest home.

If you the sick have visited, or to the thirsty given drink,
Tomorrow, there, before His Face, Truth will have drunk the wine you gave.

Yunus Emre, in this world they say but two immortals live;
Like Hizir and Ilyās, it seems, are they who drink the Stream of Life.

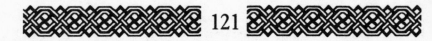 

Love of my homeland calls me – *there* would I be, crying 'O my Friend'.
Who reaches it will never leave; there would I stay, crying 'O my Friend'.

Come Azraīl and seize me for that journey where no horse may serve;
But let me mount the wooden steed and travel, crying 'O my Friend'.

Fulfilment I would find alone, would be an ever open rose,
A nightingale among the flowers to sing there, crying 'O my Friend'.

Let them fashion from this length of cloth a shroud to cover me;
I would the clothes of this world shed, don others, crying 'O my Friend'.

I would travel like Mejnūn, would climb the highest mountain peaks;
I would become a candle, burning, melting, crying 'O my Friend'.

Then set a stone above my bones to stand as days and years roll on;
Let withered flesh to its own dust return while crying 'O my Friend'.

Yunus, go your Way where those who scoff share not your ecstasy;
May I at last flow into Friendship's lake – still crying 'O my Friend'.

 122

This muezzin arose, with voice uplifted gave the Call to Prayer;
He turned his face to majesty and made the act of will for prayer.[66]

My hands in reverence I fold, the Fātiha my tongue recites;
I stoop in worship of the Truth – the bow that is prescribed for prayer.

My place of quiet retreat is like the Mount of Sinai now for me,
For there my heart has made, like Moses once, a place for joyful prayer.

My eyes there saw a form – and as, prostrate, I lay in wonderment
My total scheme of things was toppled: awe itself became my prayer.

No longer might I pray by rote, in numbers tell my rosary;
The love of *You* is now for me the end of fivefold daily prayer

See what it has made of Yunus; glorious tidings he has brought;
As lover now his converse with the Loved One two-way flows in prayer.

Engulfed by fire of Love I walk, blood-hued, for all the world to see;
No more is mind, nor mindlessness: come, see what Love has made of me.

One moment I am dust upon the Road – the next, as breezes free;
And now, a flowing brook become: come, see what Love has made of me.

I am a foaming mountain stream; my Being writhes in agony;
Weeping, as I recall my Sheykh: come, see what Love has made of me.

My eyes with tears of blood are filled; a stone is set where heart should be;
You sufferers, you know my state; come, see what Love has made of me.

O raise me by the hand – O bring me to You, where I long to be;
*You* made me weep – let me now smile: come, see what Love has made of me.

From every tongue I seek to find a Sheykh in every land I flee;
But who, in exile, knows my state? Come, see what Love has made of me.

As Mejnūn once, so now I roam; in dreams alone my Love I see;
And, waking, am brought low again: come, see what Love has made of me.

Poor Yunus I, now wholly spent; from head to foot my body rent;
Far, far from Friendship's lands now sent: come, see what Love has made of me.

With Love intense we longed for Him, and once again that Soul we found
Which, he who makes his own, is by his body wrapped as by a cloak.

When He this form has entered, every work by Him is perfect made;
And He may tell the jewel that He is within an outward form.

We know the outward forms as stalls laid out along this world's bazaar;
Yet only those who are within the stall can sell what it contains.

Many there are deceive themselves and claim that they have wares for sale;
But He it is Who gives – as He Who takes – and counts not what is loss.

Yunus, you yourself from Self, from Soul are never separate:
If you within yourself can find Him not, where is He to be found?

 125

Who trade in Love, their souls are all their capital;
I saw how great the cost to those who souls destroy.

*He* is a hero who for others gives his life;
Can sword destroy who is in righteousness arrayed?

See One in all; in who is least the saint perceive;
Think not that those are dead who wear the dervish cloth.

Swift is the Way to loftiest place on high for those
Who in true faith abide, like Jesus, thousandfold.

And swiftly they descend to lowest place beneath,
Those who exploit the world, like Ka'ārun, thousandfold.

The one who truly loves will in this sign be seen:
He will be censured, but hide not what he believes.

Fine silks he has discarded, common cloth put on,
Who hears the mystery of Ibrahim Edhem.

Keep far away from you all intellectual pride;
For God receives the one who folds another's shroud.

You all have heard it told how Mansūr, when he saw
The Truth, called: 'I am Truth' – and to the flames was thrown.

You it was who burned him, cast his ashes out;
Is this the treatment meet for those who have loved you?

Take heed, take heed, O Yunus, vaunt not: 'I have seen' –
The end is fiery flame of such as make that claim!

In former time the fire of Love was burning, too, within my soul;
I made no show of it, though well I knew the Friend had placed it there.

Those who only in the Four Books read find not the cure for Love:
Not Bey, nor Sultan, neither Judge – nor Teachers of Theology!

The earth, the sky, move in their courses, storms and tempest sway; but not
That soul shall in the end be shaken which in Love is strongly wrought.

Though I may burn a thousand times upon this Road I am content;
Sweeter by far than sugar, and most lovely, is the taste of Love.

Love is not of human mother born, and is a slave to none;
But every friend and every enemy is subject to Love's rule.

Those who are by Love made mad, of loss and profit are made free;
They fear no more the bitterness of cold, nor know the fiery heat.

From everlasting I have known the recitation 'En el Hāk,'[67]
Thou yet Mansūr, he of Baghdad, had not been sent into this world.

Who falls into the hands of Love must face his fate – be found at fault:
And so it is the name of wretched Yunus is of ill report.

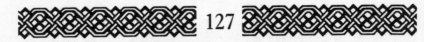 

Once more the vision of His Face I saw; again my heart was seared;
O Friend, the fire of loving You has burned into my inmost soul.

He who sees Your beauty face to face, who gives his heart to You,
Who holds the title-deed to Love, can never know satiety.

Your essence, gem-like, radiant; the sun's own purity Your Face;
Your Words for us are sugar-sweet; in awe we stand in sight of You.

Vagrant was this heart in me, my body nothing more than flesh;
Your Face I saw – my inner and my outer self were dressed in light.

Yunus Emre, wanderer – he lives in hope Your Face to see;
His gaze, unmoved, to You is turned: now fire-consumed what once was he.

 128

Since when I saw the vision of that One who is the world's Beloved
My heart, my soul, to Him I gave; His Love companion is to me.

My heart, my soul, insistently proclaim that each is slave to Him;
How shall I know which one is truly His when each with other strives?

I know that my contentment has its place between these warring two;
And though I have no counsellor, in Him I know my happiness.

If I should the condition tell of those who are in love with Him:
Held by the halter of His Love they are more gentle than the lamb.

My harmony with Him, though brief – a thousand years are not so sweet;
A day without Him passed is like a great gash, where my heart had been.

I turn and look – see, He is once again in everything that is:
Before, behind, on right, on left – what then was Winter now is Spring.

Before Hizir, Ilyās, appeared to me, I mocked undying life –
Then, where was neither food nor drink, both I received abundantly.

How many heroes, lion-like, stiffen their necks against Love's might,
And raging at the fetters of Your Love are yet made tractable!

For in the heart of every Being of all worlds is found His Love;
Who loves Him not with all his heart – know that his faith is hard as stone.

There is not one may not be set alight by but a spark from You;
Your flames once licked poor Yunus – and to all he was revealed.

Rejoice, my heart, who once knew joy – walk now, again, in peacefulness;
Fear not, to none make favour free; walk free of sorrow, free of care.

Look on the Truth of things; is not the self sufficient enemy?
Walk then in present readiness to struggle with the self you own.

The self it is which brings temptation to the traveller on this Road;
With others what have you to do? Walk untrammelled by the self.

If you should look to find security from this world's wickedness,
The dervish robe put on, and walk abandoning all pride and hate.

If you would wish to know intoxication everlasting here,
Fill to the brim the cup of Love – and walk a twelvemonth drunkenly.

Another's vineyard enter not, nor gather roses not your own;
But walk with your Beloved in *His* garden – there pluck what you will.

Be not a thorn in others' hearts; in lodges[68] be not unripe, raw;
The raw is savourless – become as food for all, cooked in Love's flame.

Yunus, yours are words of joy; your Meaning is for those who hear;
Your counsel safe delivered to all people, go your Way in joy.

Yet again Your Love intoxicates – and leaves me desolate;
Its heat has seared my heart, made of my breast meat for an offering.

As branches under snow my back it bows – I grieve unceasingly;
It makes of me a bow which from the viol draws sweet songs of pain.

Count not it shame to me, O lovers, that I sorrow though I love;
Whatever I may do – or you may do – is as our God ordains.

While yet with eyes alone I saw, I could not grasp what grieved me so;
I now know what reduces me to ash is Separation's flame.

You jurist – what you seek is to be found when you on Truth rely;
Many are they to whom, as now to Yunus, God has made His cry.

 131

While on the world I gazed I came upon the wondrous mystery;
See then your Self within yourself, as I the Friend have seen in me.

As one who serves I looked – I looked within myself and saw that One
Who on this form had life bestowed, the One Who is at one with me.

The Will it was led me to Him; if I were 'He', where might 'I' be?
No more distinction was – He I became: no 'I' remained, nor 'He'!

For the Beloved is one with me, there is no hair's-breadth difference;
Why take the distant journey when the Friend within myself I see?

Blessed has my journey proved that to this place I now have come;
The common way – I need it not: from such distraction set me free.

The Negative can hear Him not – His soul is sensed by those who grieve;
Of them I sing – from Love's rose-garden as a nightingale I came.

Mansūr was I upon that time; because of him I travelled here;
My atoms rose to Heaven's dome as I the 'I am Truth'[69] became.

Not in fire may I be burned nor on the scaffold yield my breath;
Let me, my task accomplished here, attain to bliss – for this I came.

Possessing nothing, everything I give; all time and space is mine;
For east and west and north and south, all earth and Heaven I confine.

My heart cannot receive the one who cries that form is merely dust;
For I have seen the essence of this dust with Majesty combine.

My self at last has found my Self; and this because I saw the Truth;
My fear was till the finding – free from fear no more do I repine.

Yunus, He Who brings you death, it is the Giver takes again;
And now the knowledge Who is Governor of every soul is mine.

Sainthood such an ocean is, to take the pearl deep in that sea,
To plunge into its depths, none other than a lover must you be.

We dived once more into that sea: it is the Jeweller Himself
Can tell the worth of such a pearl as we have made recovery.

Be silent sooner than be middleman to sell another's wares;
Like Ali, upright must you be who would perceive this mystery.

Mohammed understood the Truth, within himself the Truth perceived;
Truth is prepared, in every place, to show Itself to eyes that see.

It is with that authority which lovers hold I speak to all:
They who would steadfast stand let them be moved by generosity.

The learned labour, adding black to white, and piling tome on tome;
The chapters of *this* book read in the hearts of all humanity.

Go your way, O Sufi, hypocrite who trades in things for show;
Who but the Truth alone may give His servants their necessity?

The Truth has place in human hearts; His signs are seen in the Koran;
Above the Throne of Heaven alone Love's turrets rise more loftily.

Say then that I am mad, cannot discern today from yesterday;
It is because the arrow from Love's bow has struck this heart in me.

Come now, Yunus the forlorn, grasp here the hem of sainthood's robe;
For every wretchedness, in naughting self is the sure remedy.

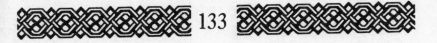 

Who sees, as I have seen, his Lover, the Beloved of all the world,
Will find Him in his madness, in the mountains, having lost himself.

Who loses self with thankfulness in searching for a sight of Him –
How could it be that, seeing Him, he could be blinded? God forbid!

Who is there with tongue to tell the Beauty His creation is?
Save of the soul alone, what lips the savour of His Words may taste?

Whatever is by us beloved, that it is our tongue must tell;
So, whether or not I will, I speak the Word of Him Who holds my heart.

Wherever he may be, whose tongue the sweetness of His words recites
Will bring His loveliness, His grace, to all the nations of the earth.

He forces not His Friendship's Love on any who desire it not;
He set the lovers' star to shine above Affection's lofty tower.

My words are as an echo off the rock to those who sorrow not;
My fellow sufferer it is who comprehends my mystery.

Who gives himself to You in Love, his soul lives in eternity;
His prayers Your Love encompasses, each moment day and night.

If it had been that Venus in the sky had seen what Yunus saw,
Her lute she would put by, forget – her harp her hand would stroke no more.

This God of mine has with His Love made of my breast a wounded head;
He made my heart His own and to the world exposed my mystery.

Within my heart He walks with me; with me He speaks upon my tongue;
This God a vision to my eyes appears as His celestial light.

The eyes that are the soul's see Him, its tongue it is His tidings tell;
For He it is dwells in my heart, has made of it His heavenly throne.

His light it is lights up the soul, a place He has in every heart,
That hearts and souls alike in everyone should overflow with Love.

He proffers to each soul His cup for each to drink it to the dregs;
I drank that brimming cup – such drunkenness my soul had never known.

It is in that intoxication that our language pours out pearls –
The jewels of that God Whose Love has brought me to the dervish Way.

How may I make good a claim to be a dervish, slave to Truth?
But hundred thousands like to me has Love made mantle-bearers too.

So Yunus still consoles himself, delights that he has seen the Friend;
His love the lodges of the saints makes ring with revelry and joy.

Cup-bearer fill the cup, and bring to us who drink the wine of Love;
Let Doctors of the Law, too, drink of that which is to us our need.

Of God is our discourse in Love; our wine the waters of Kevser;
Our King, the King of Kings – of Separation is our song.

Let loving discourse be, to check the Teachers of Theology;
That God-like state *we* seek who drinks of which will share eternity.

The robe and cap point not the Way, nor in the cloak is Wisdom found;
If you hold not religion's Truth search not, in vain, the page profound.

Seventy volumes have you read – and piety you show in this;
But if it be not seen in deed – then read again, a hundred years.

A thousand times you went on pilgrimage, a hundred years lived pure?
If you one heart have harmed – go, travel for another hundred more!

Ask then of me to know which is the best – the Ka'āba, or the heart;
I give the heart my choice, for there I know the Truth has made His home.

Hearts of his neighbours were entrusted to His Messenger[70] by Truth;
It was upon the Night of the Ascent,[71] the Friend this Word made known.

For you, Yunus, it is decreed – hold to humility by its skirt;
If purity you seek, remain for ever in the human heart.

 136

No need have they of wooden craft who throw themselves into Love's sea;
O God, where elsewhere may we find such intercourse – such moment sweet?

All sadness put aside – lament not: 'In this world I have no part.'
Once you have loved the One Beloved no more may sorrow seize your heart.

And if you too had seen that One Beloved Whom I have seen and loved,
No more to others would you give advice – but would this life give up.

The one who loves knows not advice, no profit can he see in it;
All calculation throw away – all rancour and all pride forget.

For they who truly lovers are, His sign upon their face is seen –
The tears which day and night, unceasingly, with His compassion stream.

A faith abides which lovers in all lands have ever owned – and own;
But those who live in lovelessness, that faith, by God, have never known.

Yunus, lift not your face from dust which lovers of all times have trod;
Your life a hundred thousand times give up – in this shall you find God.

Does not the radiance of Truth descend on lovers ceaselessly?
Are they not dispossessed of Truth on whom that radiance falls not?

Know the sign by which is known the heart which is of all the Heart;
Is it not this: a Road which open lies from all hearts to that Heart?

If in a single cage they put together crow and nightingale
Are these not always melancholy made each from the other's song?

And when the crow implores for separation from the nightingale
Is that, by God, not what the nightingale itself would most desire?

And so the case is likewise as between the wise and foolish ones;
Is it not known that to the ignorant their faith is ignorance?

Counsel not a lover – conflict every time will surely flow;
And that advice is flawed when given by the letter of the Law.

The wise will comprehend the Word which two-and-seventy nations speak;
And does not every word which wretched Yunus speaks to you ring true?

 138

Your Love has torn me from my self; You are my need, and You alone;
Day and night I am afire; You are my need, and You alone.

Possessions bring me no delight, nor am I grieved by poverty;
My consolation is Your Love – You are my need, and You alone.

Your Love brings death[72] to lovers – plunges them into Your sea of Love;
Such death transfiguration brings: You are my need, and You alone.

May I drink of Your wine of Love, like Mejnūn scale the mountain peak;
My heart now yearning day and night; You are my need, and You alone.

Discourse in Love – the Sufi need, and for the saints the Latter Day;
As lovers their beloved need – You are my need, and You alone.

Should they put me to death – my atoms as they rise up to the skies
Will, though but dust, cry out to You: 'You are my need, and You alone.'

Yunus Emre still my name; each day burns higher still the flame;
In both the worlds my only claim: 'You are my need, and You alone.'

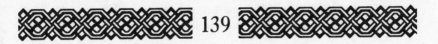 139

Of that cup-bearer's wine we drank Whose tavern is the Throne of Heaven;
We were made drunk by Him Whose beaker is the souls of humankind.

Those whom the fire of Love consumes, their Being is made radiant;
That flame is other than the fires of earth or hell – no hurt it gives.

The prayer recited in our drunken fellowship is 'En el Hāk';[73]
A thousandfold we are as Mansūr was – and no less mad than he!

This congregation of our hearts makes food and drink for humankind;
That Light which burns in us – the sun and moon are moths around its flame.

The topers in our fellowship are as Shah Edhem, man of sacrifice;
So may a hundred thousand cities now, like Balkh, in ruins lie.

Yunus, speak not ever words of ecstasy to heedless ones;
For you know well how all their days and nights are passed in times like these.

Those who are dumb are they who have fit tidings for the deaf to hear;
The soul alone it is can understand the words of deaf and dumb.

So speaking not we understood – and strove when understanding failed:
Humility the treasure is of the true dervish on this Road.

We loved, we were the Lover; loved in turn, we then were the Beloved;
Each instant we are born anew – how can such freshness ever pall?

When seventy-two dispute together each is sundered from the next;
We look on each, but criticize not any – be they of rank, or none.

Yunus, do you seek a saint? Heaven and earth are filled with these:
Within each stone and grain of sand, in thousands – Moses, Imran's son.

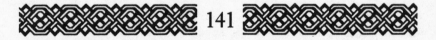 

How is it that you nurture, cherish so, this frame of yours, this form?
Forget not Resurrection while you taste the pleasures of this world.

Should ostentation be the mark of those whose outer form is earth?
From earth you were created and to earth again will you return.

He is not of sound mind, but mad, who raises lofty palaces;
The work of every man to rubble must return within a span.

Yet strive, and earn, feed self – but others too; a heart to people bring;
And rather than a hundred Ka'ābas, visit *once* the heart of Man.

Who claims to deal in miracles, who makes a show of holiness –
Let such his self make Moslem; that is miracle enough to plan.

The one whose self is God-surrendered travels straightly on Truth's Way,
With morrow finds Mohammed intercedes – will not be turned away.

Yet though in thousands prophets come, by intercession who is shriven?
For woe to us if God's benevolence were not so freely given.

Yunus, rest in that Reality in which all has its ground;
In worship joined with all that is – in that true saintliness is found.

 142

Lawful the lover's blood has been decreed by him for the Beloved;
The Loved One from His own design recites – the lover His Koran.

Once separated from the Loved One, better by the rope to die;
The lover's throat is ever haltered with the cord He has prepared.

The lover's eye can never lose the vision of the One Beloved;
And so Zuleika needs must see in Joseph symbol of the Real.

True life, for those who love, is dying on the Road to the Beloved;[74]
If they should ask of me I give this as the evidence of Love.

Long time ago it was when Solomon and Belkis lovers were;
And even these were helpless in the search to find a cure for Love.

For Love it was Harūt and Marūt came to earth from skies above;
When they had seen the face of Venus, they forgot the Merciful.[75]

Think never Love contemptible – to whomsoever It has called:
Of rulers It has even ruled their heads – and hearth and home destroyed.

So Ferhād in the course of Love his self put to the utmost test;
And for the sake of Shirīn his beloved Husrev, too, gave his life.

The tale of Leylā and Mejnūn gives wonderment to all the world;
And Abd ur-Razzāk, holy one, for Love his very faith forsook.

Yunus sorrows that time's fleeting faithfulness must be so brief;
To find the constant Lover yields his soul – this is the end of grief.

109

It is to us mysterious how first the Friend looked fair on us;
His loving gaze upon the city of my Being rested then.

I could not, if I would, turn from His Face these my adoring eyes;
For he, with sweetest Word, has made my heart a fire of Love for Him.

Of whomsoever I their counsel seek all bid me patient be;
But see how flames of Love the curtain of my patience have consumed.

In that which *I* may will should come to pass, shall patience bring success?
For in my soul my Friend a Soul has left behind with His caress.

The states of loving and of being loved – morrow will sunder these;
Now all my care is for today: for *this* what may the morrow teach?

It is for this that Yunus loves the Friend with all that in him is:
All souls their true Love seek – sink in whatever is adored by each.

 144

O lovers, where my soul has sojourned is beyond my power to tell;
Not by my tongue can I reveal the One Who took hold of my heart.

My tongue cannot contain that fullness of the heart by lovers known;
How much has overflowed and poured away is felt by heart alone.

Think not it shame that they may joy who have been grieved by pain of Love;
That they find happiness who in their faithlessness have found their faith.

For those who lovers are – to laugh, to weep, to be alive, to die,
To be reviled of men or favoured – these are one, a means of joy.

A sacrifice to Love for all, Yunus by Love is wordless made;
Let him be trampled on – but never into separation fade.

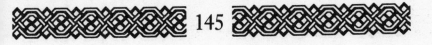 

I would a question ask of you who own the dervish brotherhood:
What have the Sheykhs of former times been pleased to say of this our Way?

Grant to our question your reply that through your Word we may find grace;
Through rays by which Its hearth is known, to whom may Love reveal Its place?

'The first door is – observe the negative command which is the Law;
Each syllable of the Koran shall serve to wash away your sins.

The second, is the Way – to bind the self in service due to all;
The Master will absolve all they who on the true Path find their Way.

The third is Learning – with it open wide the eyes of heart and soul;
The palace of true Meaning is sublime, like to the Throne of Heaven.

And fourthly, Holy Truth: this never can be lacking in a saint;
With It your days are festivals, your nights become the Night of Power.'[76]

The Law is harsh; the Way of dervishhood is rock-strewn too, and steep;
The path of Learning is precipitous – the highest point is Truth.

The dervish post is where he is encompassed by the four great gates;
That place from which, wherever he may look, his night is turned to day.

A dervish who comes there will make discovery of both the worlds;
And there the Master of all Masters will, with praises, welcome him.

For dervish in the state of fourfold ecstasy death brings no pain;[77]
Not to that stage along the Way will sluggard travellers attain.

Together, forty men can scarce drag down a tree from mountain top;
Which then of these among our band of saints will cross the Sirāt bridge?

When you your irreligion cast away claim not for self true faith;
Else shall it be you smash the stew pot – strew the stew upon the ground!

Four are the gates, and forty places, sixty-and-a-hundred stages
Of that state which opens at the last to dervish Friends of God.

Yunus, the lover, tells not that to you which is impossible –
This poet, old in years, the face of Meaning to all men reveals.

111

I am he who weeps before that Lover's face,
Who willingly surrenders soul to his Beloved.

In rapturous awe throughout each night till dawn am I
Waiting, before the Lover's Face, expectantly.

And when the light of morning comes still am I sad;
As though I were a nightingale among Love's blooms.

Since when my soul was taken hold by Love Divine,
I am become a wanderer, like to Mejnūn.

A moth made mad by radiance from that Beauty's light,
My wings, my body, wholly by Its fire consumed.

Since when I drank a draught of His sweet wine of Love
He penetrates my depth, the wound that is my heart.

Today upon Love's Road with Mansūr – I am one;
There may I walk till to his scaffold I, too, come.

I am the love-lorn nightingale among Love's flowers
Who would to every heart bring tidings of that Love.

Yunus the lover now in lands afar must dwell,
An exile, that to strangers he his Love might tell.

The Lord a marketplace has made within the hearts of brotherhood;
Many like us were found in that bazaar as they passed on the Road.

The brethren, taking wing, in flight passed over mountains, over plains;
They fell into Love's seething cauldron, there were made fit nourishment.

This world of ours is like a body left unburied by the Way;
Curs fall upon the corpse: the friend of Truth, let free, no more need stay.

May I to them who have not sacrificed their lives give lover's name?
The lover is the one whose life is made to be a cause for blame.

Since he again saw Taptūk's face Yunus once more is stupefied –
Though from his lake all but a cordial cup he to himself denied.

 148

In whatsoever face I look I see my Taptūk's radiance;
I have today known what I sought. 'Tomorrow' – what is that to me?

Tomorrow is for me today – a wedding day, a festival;
A voice comes to me in a dream: hearken to the news it brings.

These are the tidings of the Friend: 'Make Self the Beloved for your self;'
Look to the Friend – to Him the city of your Being dedicate.

Save to the one who Being has attained, the Truth to none is known;
It is within this Being that the Friend reveals His Face to us.

I saw the Face of sainthood and abandoned all uncertainty;
Then came to Friendship's garden – saw there flowers whose like I seek to tell.

The Friend's Face is to me a rose; a nightingale my Love for Him;
No more by hesitation bound now I the saint of Love have found.

Since from the Truth the cry is made: 'Am I not truly Lord to you?'[78]
The faithful ones their affirmation gave, and so confessed their faith.

Then, Yunus, from the faithless realms there came reproaches without cease;
My Sultan, truly Saintly One, from hempen girdle[79] give release.

Scorn not the dervish if to faith and to religion you make claim;
The world entire stands longingly to catch a glimpse of dervish-hood.

Moon and sun, expectant, crave the discourse of the dervishes,
While angels tell their rosary as they recite of dervish-hood.

Nazarenes repentant stand, and thrones forever lose their power;
The hills and rocks prostrate themselves before the sight of dervish-hood.

The dervish arrow flies afar, it pierces instantly the soul;
Be ever watchful, ready stand: think never naught of dervish-hood.

Faithful in all, His Love is peace, Who is the Glory of the World;[80]
If you through Him seek constancy – beware you mock not dervish-hood.

Should you bring harm on them your life will wither and your days be short;
Sightless will you wander till your eyes discover dervish-hood.

The earth and sky the robe obliterates, yet may their worth endure;
The Lord and cup-bearer now one, His Love makes drunk all dervish-hood.

Though you may read a thousand times a day the Four Books brought from
     Heaven,
In Truth you may not see His Face save that your heart loves dervish-hood.

Yunus calls: 'My soul was dead; this Love brought it to life again;
No more in me is "I" and "You" when we shall witness dervish-hood.'

Hear, O my beloved ones, they of the brotherhood are come;
Let us give our hearts in thanks: the brotherhood to us is come.

He whose eye has seen the Face forgets forever self-regard,
Sings only of the hidden world: behold the brotherhood is come.

The dervishes are birds in flight, are drunkards at the feast of Truth,
Are bearers of prosperity: behold the brotherhood is come.

The dervishes know tenderness – who see them cast their wits away;
Their secrets are above the Heavens: behold the brotherhood is come.

From the land of holy Balūm,[81] from whose lips sweet sugar flows;
From the garden of the Friend – behold the brotherhood is come.

Yunus, your servant, without hope, with none to help him, stood alone;
Yet let our lives be sacrifice: behold the brotherhood is come.

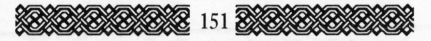 151

What passion was it brought me to this dervish non-conformity?[82]
When naught of care I had within my heart the realm of life was there.

When That it was Which filled my heart, and was discovered by my soul;
The Loved One in this city dwelt and was a guest within my home.

Then was the time, that blessed time, when sorrow was not, neither woe;
When naught of care I had within my heart in that same land of life.

We pastured in the fields of light; the Word divine we spoke to all;
And joyfulness in Friendship found together in the house of power.

We took our rest around the Throne of Heaven, our shade celestial light;
Our very souls were made there one with his – the Chosen One[83] of God.

No pen was there, no written Word, nor eighteen thousand worlds like this;
And in that moment neither Eve nor Adam yet had name or fame.

A pretext brought us to this realm which we beheld in majesty;
Our journey we begin again – ahead the homeland of our hearts.

Huseyn it was, and Mansūr too, who saw the form in timelessness
And offered self to Truth – the tumult reached the borders of Baghdad!

Yunus, the time has come – forsake your life today on Friendship's Way
That, where before it once had been, you may rest in Eternity.

I climbed along the plum tree branch and there I ate the grapes I saw;
The orchard owner called to me: 'Why eat you of my walnut store?'

To me he kindness showed, but in return I gave him calumny;
The passing pedlar shouted: 'See, you took the best fruit of his tree.'

An earthen brick I placed within the pot – the north wind boiled it dry;
The clay I dipped in water, gave to those who asked what I did try.

To the weaver thread I gave – he wound it not into a ball;
In truth, in truth, let those who place an order for their cloth take all.

I loaded on the backs of forty mules a sparrow's tiny wing;
They had not strength to draw the plough – and so remained the days of Spring.

A house-fly swooped upon an eagle flying, struck it to the ground;
No lie is this I tell to you, but truth – I saw the dust whirl round.

I wrestled with a paralytic, yet by my foot he gained the throw;
Though hard I struggled I could not avail – he made me inward glow.

Down from the mountain heights of Kāf above a rock at me they raced;
As it came crashing to the road below, my face it near defaced.

The fish climbed up the poplar tree the pickled pitch of it to taste;
The stork gave birth – a donkey's foal was born – ponder, not in haste.

I whispered to the sightless one – the deaf one heard that word I spoke;
The dumb one shouted – mine was the word he uttered when the silence broke.

An ox I strangled, knocked it over, on the ground I threw it down;
The owner of the ox complained that I had caused his goose to drown.

Again I could not save myself, I could not know what I should do;
Another pedlar cried: 'My glowing ember has been filched by you.'

I quarrelled with a tortoise and a fellow traveller with no eye;
I asked their journey's end – 'As far as Kayseri,' they made reply.

Yunus speaks this Word – no other Word there is resembles It:
For so he veils the Face of Meaning from the mind of hypocrite.[84]

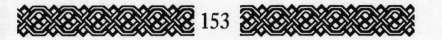 

You who say to me that I pray not, know that I pray indeed;
Whether or no in ritual form my prayer is made God knows my need.

None alone save God can tell who Moslem is, who infidel;
As He cures my inconstancy my prayer in Truth I tell.

This frailty surpasses rule, drinks of the wine of inner Truth;
It raises from the eyes of life the veil – and wipes my tears away.

The Friend is here for all to see: full clear I saw His Face revealed;
No greater place than this the end of all who read in Wisdom's book.

The wise of this world use their sharply pointed words, in commentary;
My words mysterious they cannot sift through forms explanatory.

Perceive my inner Word; give news of Him who is Unsymbolized;
And ask of grieving lovers if my words, born too of grief, be true.

In grief is cure for lovers' pain; as lovers, sorrowing, yet are rich.
Who hear my cry, they know the voice of Power – and they tell of it.

Who seeks the Friend, let him draw near to me that I may make Him known;
From first to last my Word is this: the nature of myself I own.

Yunus, speak the Truth, though yet the Negative no right admit;
Prepare, safeguard, the food of Truth – the wise will taste the salt of it.

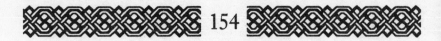 

O friends, who ever heard of lovers who repented of their love;
Or knew a flame take hold when fiery brand was flung into the sea?

My King, your fire of Love fell in the ocean of our human hearts;
They wonder when from seething waters Wisdom bursts into the world.

Jesus and Moses, thousandfold, in wonderment walk in Your Love;
They stand amazed that I am swallowed too by Love's leviathan.

Let not God's servant plunge into this sea who knows not how to swim;
So deep the ocean of God's Love, strange would it be should he not sink.

He takes a jewel for a bead who has not learned the gem-smith's craft;
And knowing not the price which it may bring he barters it for naught.

The one who here has never seen the Face of Truth in clarity
Will on the morrow wander, searching, seeking in bewilderment.

Yunus proclaims he is Man's slave, and Taptūk image of the Friend;
Who holds not that this Word we speak is true shall yet pursue their end.

You it is I love deep in this life itself;
No pillared place, to which my Path can lead, more deep.

In everything I see You are – to overflowing;
Where then shall I place You than myself more deep?

He stands Beloved of all the world – unsymbolized;
Can symbol be of Symbol that is yet more deep?

Ask not of me from me – for I am not in 'me';
Within my covering cloth an empty form lies deep.

My reach falls short of Him Who took me from myself;
From where my Sultan stands can any go more deep?

Some there were who in transfiguration shared;
But some there are reach out to That Which is more deep.

Who by that beam is touched which streams from Love's own sun
Is of a flame possessed – sun's ray is not so deep.

Love of You has seized the 'Me' from out of me;
How sweet that pain which in its cure should lie so deep.

The Law, the Way, are paths for those who so arrive;
The Truth, and Wisdom, are than each of these more deep.

They said the speech of birds was known to Solomon;
There is a Solomon – than Solomon more deep.

All creed, and all religion, I have now forgot;
What doctrine this, which even more than creed lies deep?

They say he faithless is who casts away his creed;
What faithlessness is this, when faith lies not so deep?

In journeying has Yunus come upon that Friend
Who at the portal stands – which is than Self more deep.

 156

Long was it I searched for God; now I have found Him, what of that?
By day and night my tears have flowed; if now I smile, what then of that?

Once, upon the brethren's polo-field I was a whirling ball;
If now I have become my Sultan's polo-stick – why, what of that?

I was a handful of red roses where the saints held discourse sweet;
From hand to hand my blooms were passed – if they have faded, what of that?

The wise, the Doctors of the Law, in schools have found what they have sought;
If I made my discovery in dissolution – what of that?

Give ear, give ear, to Yunus: once again he is a man possessed;
If I have plunged into the depths of sainthood's Meaning – what of that?

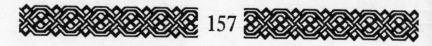 

If so it be, O God, You call me to account,
This is how I, there, shall make reply to You.

Myself it was that I oppressed and sinned against;
Has what I ever did brought harm, O Lord, to You?

You involved my dust in guilt before I came;
Before I yet was born Adam rebelled, through You.

From everlasting only You made me rebel;
The Voice which all creation fills comes but from You.

What had You planned for me, so full of ill, my God;
For was it *I* who ordered me? Not so, but You.

My eyes I opened – prison cell behind locked door –
Self, brimful of lust – the Devil's works I saw.

Lest of starvation I should die within that cell,
Of pure and of unclean I ate as need befell.

Yet was there ever any time You shared in dearth?
Could *my* will ever overbear Your own on earth?

Do You recall that You were ever famished too
If I ate what You gave – or I caused want to You?

You stretch the bridge[85] that I must pass fine as a hair,
And ask that I myself should save *me* from Your snare.

Has Man the means to cross a bridge set in the sky?
His only courses are to stay, or fall – or fly!

Your servants too build bridges – but of charity –
The good that is of *helping* travellers on their Way.

Firm they build them, strengthen them for every need,
That they who travel on their Way may know God speed!

The scales[86] are poised by You to measure ill desire;
It seems it is Your will to throw me on the fire.

Such scales are fit for grocery – are but a tool
That's proper to the trades of those who seek to fool.

As sin is much the foulest of the foul; at last
Before Your presence, profit comes from wrong that's passed.

It is Your part my sin to cover with Your Grace;
What need to weigh in scales my evil's every trace?

You it is Who sets the scene that into flames I fall;
And God forbid in this to see the Lord of All!

You are the Seer Who perceives my every state;
What need of scales to know of all my works the weight?

Are You still unrevenged when I am called by death,
My body brought to rot – my eyes stuffed full of earth?

Was hand of Yunus ever cause of hurt to You
When evident, and hidden – both – are in Your view?

What need is served now for a handful of Your dust
By fractious talk – O Lord most Mighty, and most Just?

# NOTES

1. For Moslems the Revealed Books are the Torah and the Psalms, the Gospel of Jesus, and the Koran.
2. Text *Eren, see* Glossary.
3. *See* SOLOMON in Glossary.
4. Text 'Love is our imam . . .'; *see* IMAM in Glossary.
5. Text *Dost, see* Glossary. Occurs *passim* in these poems.
6. Text '. . . is our Kiblē', *see* Glossary.
7. Moslems are enjoined to pray at five fixed times each day, apart from supererogatory prayer.
8. *See* Note 40.
9. The Koran refers to the balances of individual good and evil works being struck on the Day of Judgement.
10. *See* as-SIRĀT in Glossary.
11. Text *Hāk, see* Glossary. This use of 'Truth' for 'God' occurs *passim* in these poems.
12. *See* Note 1 above.
13. Text *Elif, see* Glossary.
14. Analogue for wickedness: see Old Testament, Book of Esther.
15. Text *Sheri'āt, see* Glossary.
16. Text *Tārikāt, see* Glossary.
17. To some formalists the dervish is culpable for his seeming unorthodoxy.
18. *See* Note 15.
19. Allusion to the Prophet Mohammed's saying: 'Die before you die.'
20. Allusion to the Prophet Mohammed's saying: 'Who knows himself knows his Lord.'
21. Text *Mevlāna, see* Glossary.
22. A dervish (*see* Glossary) contemporary with Yunus Emre, given his name 'Geyikli' ('of the deer') because wild deer followed him.
23. *See* SOLOMON in Glossary.
24. Text *Rahman, see* Glossary.
25. The Koranic account of Abraham's obedience to God's command to sacrifice his son, and His intervention at the last moment, leaves unmentioned the son's name. Moslems accept that the son was Ismaīl who was Abraham's first son.

26. *See* KADIR GEJESI in Glossary.
27. Refers to the ritual ablution before, and to the prostration in, the formal prayer.
28. Text *Ijāzet, see* Glossary.
29. *See* SOLOMON in Glossary.
30. *See* Note 1.
31. Text *Imam, see* Glossary.
32. *See* SOLOMON in Glossary.
33. Text *Dost, see* Glossary.
34. Young babies were washed in salt for strengthening.
35. *See* MUNKIR (and NEKIR) in Glossary.
36. *See* Note 10.
37. Text *Elif, see* Glossary.
38. *See* SOLOMON in Glossary.
39. *See* MIR'ĀJ in Glossary.
40. Reference to Sura (Chapter) 7.175 of the Koran: 'When God created the souls of humankind He asked them: "Am I not your Lord?", and they replied: "Indeed we so witness," as a testament and covenant.'
41. *See* Note 1.
42. *See* MANSŪR al-HALLĀJ in Glossary.
43. Mythical mount Kaf, traditionally reputed to be in the Caucasus, the dwelling of the Simurgh. *See* SOLOMON in Glossary. Hamza was the Prophet's uncle and the name is used synonymously with courage.
44. *See* MIR'ĀJ in Glossary.
45. Refers to a parable in which one of a band of forty dervishes, to illustrate the unity of their being, held out his arm so that a wound inflicted on him caused blood to flow from all forty.
46. *See* Note 43.
47. Letters of the Arabic alphabet. *See also* Note 55.
48. Not Yunus the poet, but the prophet Jonah.
49. *See* Note 14.
50. The four elements of the universe.
51. Alludes to, by quotation from, Sura (Chapter) 55.26 of the Koran: 'All [that exists] will pass away – save the Countenance of our Lord of Glory and Honour.'
52. *See* Note 35.
53. The 'Upper Lands' are considered by some to refer to the regions of the Caucasus, including what is now northern Iran, northern Azerbaijan, and Armenia.
54. Before being shrouded for burial bodies would normally be washed in warm water.
55. Cities of the Seljuk domains, now in Turkey, Iran and Azerbaijan.

56. Three letters of the Arabic alphabet. Other similar groups of letters come at the beginning of several chapters of the Koran. Their meaning is accepted by the generality of commentators as unknown.

57. An alternative reading would be: 'I made my day(light) into night;' but the sense borne by the words in past centuries has been preferred.

58. *See* SHERIK in Glossary.

59. *See* Note 20.

60. *See* HĀJ in Glossary. It is of the essence of the Pilgrimage that each pilgrim avows his intent by conscious act of will. *See also* Note 66.

61. The reed flute, used in some dervish ceremonies, has mystic significance.

62. Text *Hāj*, *see* Glossary.

63. Text *Sırāt*, *see* Glossary.

64. *See* SOLOMON in Glossary.

65. Text *Burāk*, *see* Glossary.

66. Moslems make a conscious act of will, by word of mouth, before each of the five formal daily prayers.

67. *See* MANSŪR al-HALLĀJ in Glossary.

68. That is, the dervish convents, or lodges.

69. *See* MANSŪR al-HALLĀJ in Glossary.

70. The Prophet Mohammed.

71. Text *Mir'āj*, *see* Glossary.

72. *See* Note 19.

73. As at Note 69.

74. *See* Note 19.

75. *See* ar-RAHMĀN in Glossary.

76. *See* KADIR GEJESI in Glossary.

77. *See* Note 19.

78. *See* Note 40.

79. Text *Zunnār*, *see* Glossary.

80. The Prophet Mohammed.

81. A companion of Geyikli Hasan; *see* Note 22.

82. Text *Melāmet*, *see* Glossary.

83. Text *Mustafa*, *see* Glossary.

84. Some have tried to interpret this 'nonsense' poem. The last of these fourteen couplets (the final lines of every one of which rhyme in the original Turkish) is perhaps a sufficient interpretation of this Zen-like piece.

85. *See* as-SIRĀT in Glossary.

86. *See* Note 9.

# GLOSSARY

**ABD ur-RAZZĀK** Features in the *Mantiq at-Tāyyir* (*see* SOLOMON below). In that fable he is a spiritual leader at Mecca. One day he dreams he is in the land of Rūm (*see* below) and that he prostrates himself before images – a gross sin in Islam. On awakening he calls his four hundred disciples together to accompany him to the land of Rūm. Having arrived he falls desperately in love with a Christian girl taking no heed of the remonstrations of his dervishes. The girl says she will accept him if he will either burn the Koran, drink wine, or forswear his faith. He decides to drink wine; is taken to a tavern, and from there to the church. In his drunkenness he puts on Christian attire and accepts that creed. His disciples forsake him and turn back on the road to Mecca. On their return one of the dervishes who had stayed there reproaches the others for their lack of loyalty; and they set out together in search of Abd ur-Razzāk. After much prayer and petition they prevail upon him; the girl sees a vision; she becomes a Moslem.

**ALI** Cousin and son-in-law of the Prophet, and father of Hasan and Huseyn (*see* below). Was the fourth Successor (Caliph) to the Prophet. Is considered by the Shi'a branch of Islam to have been the due Successor to Mohammed.

**AZRAĪL** The Angel of Death.

**BĀKI** Things enduring and real, as distinct from things transitory and illusory; the latter being *fāni* (*see* below). Pre-eminently *bāki* is God, the only eternal, self-subsistent, Reality.

**BALKH** Known as *Umm al-Bilād* (Mother of Cities), is one of the oldest inhabited places on earth. It was the birthplace of Rūmi, was destroyed by Jenghiz Khan, and partially restored by Timur-i-Lenk (Tamerlain) about half a century after Yunus Emre.

**BARĀK** Predecessor of Taptūk (*see* below) in the line of Yunus Emre's Sheykhs (*see* below).

**BELKIS** The Queen of Sheba, wife of Solomon (*see* below).

**BURĀK** The winged steed which carried Mohammed on the Night Ascent (*see* MIR'ĀJ).

**DERVISH** A traveller by any of the many Sufi (mystic) *tārikats* (*see* below).
**DOST** Primary meaning is 'Friend'; occurs frequently in Sufi poetry either literally or, mostly, allegorically to symbolize God.

**EDHEM** *See* IBRAHIM EDHEM below.
**ELIF** Turkish spelling of the first letter of the Arabic alphabet. It has significance both as representing the language in which the Koran was revealed, and as the initial letter of the word 'Allah'. It is also the simplest letter in the alphabet – a single downward stroke.
**EREN** A Turkish word meaning 'one who arrives' or 'attains'. Used specifically of one pursuing the dervish way. In that sense is here translated by 'saint' (as in the Epistles of the New Testament) to mean a member of the community; or, in the plural, by 'brethren', 'brotherhood', or 'sainthood'.

**FĀNI** *See* BĀKI above.
**al-FĀTIHA** The Opening Sura (Chapter) of the Koran, recited at every formal prayer.
**FERHĀD (and SHIRĪN)** Lovers in a famous romance; *see* LEYLA (and MEJNŪN) below.
**FERIDŪN (and NŪSHIRVĀN)** Names synonymous with great wealth.
**FIRMĀN** A Ruler's edict or command.

**HĀJ** The pilgrimage to Mecca enjoined on every Moslem who can afford it once in his or her lifetime.
**HĀK** Absolute Truth, Right, Justice; one of the many Attributes or Names of God. (*See* also MANSŪR al-HALLĀJ below.)
**HARŪT (and MARŪT)** Two angels who, according to fable, refused to do homage to Adam. God accordingly banished them to earth. There they fell in love with a woman, and succeeded in prevailing on her by teaching her the word of power by which to ascend to Heaven; she used the word, ascended, and was transformed by God into Zuhre (the planet Venus).
**HASAN** Grandson of the Prophet being the eldest son of Ali (*see* above).
**HIZIR** A mysterious being featuring in Sura (Chapter) 18.64 seqq. of the Koran. He accompanies Moses on a journey throughout which he performs actions which on the surface are wrongful but are interpreted in each case to show the hidden purposes of God. For Sufis he is an analogue of the need for absolute, unquestioning obedience by a *murid* to his *murshīd* (*see* below). He also symbolizes God as an ever-present help in time of need. Hence also symbolizes immortality and, in this regard, is sometimes coupled with Ilyās (Elias).
**HOURI** One of the maidens who will greet true believers in Heaven, a place of gardens and running waters.
**HUSEYN** Younger son of Ali (*see* above). Killed at the battle of Kerbela by

the army of the then Caliph on the tenth day of the Moslem (lunar) month Muharrem in AD 680.

**IBRAHIM EDHEM** A king of Balkh (*see* above) who forsook all to follow the quest for truth and meaning. A supreme Sufi exemplar. Is said to have inspired the 'Abu ben Adhem, may his tribe increase ...' in the poem by Leigh Hunt.

**IJÂZET** Certificate awarded to graduates of theological colleges, and also by the Sheykh of a Sufi Order to a disciple.

**IMAM** The leader of congregational prayer in a mosque who stands in front of the rows of worshippers. He has no priestly function and may be chosen from the most devout or respected of those present.

**ISRAFĪL** The angel who will rouse the dead on Judgement Day.

**KA'ĀBA** The cube-shaped building some forty feet high in the centre of the Great Mosque at Mecca. The central point for the Hāj (*see* above).

**KA'ĀRUN** Put his trust in his wealth, so great as to have become proverbial. His downfall is referred to at Sura (Chapter) 28.76–82 of the Koran.

**KADIR GEJESI** The Turkish translation of the Arabic *Leylat al-Qadr* ('the Night of Power'). The precise date on which the night falls is not known; it is during the last ten days of the Moslem (lunar) month of Ramazan, the month of fasting. According to tradition the command to Mohammed to begin to recite the Koran was delivered by Gabriel to him on this night.

**KEVSER** Turkish form of the Arabic *al-Kauthar* meaning 'abundance'. The name of a river in Paradise, and the title of Sura 108 of the Koran.

**KIBLĒ** (Both syllables are pronounced.) The direction of Mecca to which Moslems face in prayer, marked by an apse-like niche in the wall of a mosque called the *mihrāb*.

**LEYLA** (and **MEJNŪN**) Lovers in a tale which for centuries has been part of the folklore of every Moslem country. Mejnūn's love deprives him of his reason, so that his very name is now synonymous with 'made mad by passion'. The story is an allegory of the soul's passionate yearning for union with the Divine Beloved.

**MANSŪR al-HALLĀJ** (= **Mansur the Wool-carder**) Lived some three hundred years after the Prophet Mohammed. A philosopher and mystic according to whose thought:

> God, who in essence is love, created Man after His image to the end that His creature, loving Him alone, may suffer a spiritual transformation, find the divine image in himself, and thus attain to union with the divine will and nature ... He

does not appear to have attached this meaning [that is, the doctrine of incarnation] to his own case, yet there are other parallels of an extraordinary kind which mark him out as the nearest of all Muslim mystics to the spirit of Christ.

(Chapter on 'Mysticism' in *The Legacy of Islam*, Oxford University Press; first edition, 1931.)

He uttered the words *An'al-Haqq* (in modern Turkish script this becomes *En el Hāk*) meaning 'I am the Truth'. (*See* HĀK above.) For this proclamation of the consummation of his union with the Divine he was executed at Baghdad in AD 922. His prayer before execution (translation taken from the same OUP publication already quoted) was:

And these Thy servants who are gathered to slay me, in zeal for Thy religion and in desire to win Thy favour, forgive them, O Lord, and have mercy upon them; for verily if Thou hadst revealed to them that which Thou hast revealed to me, they would not have done what they have done; and if Thou hadst hidden from me that which Thou hast hidden from them, I should not have suffered this tribulation. Glory unto Thee in whatsoever Thou doest, and glory unto Thee in whatsoever Thou willest!

**MARŪT** *See* HARŪT above.

**MEJNŪN** *See* LEYLA above.

**MELĀMET** Primary meaning is 'blame' or 'censure'. Also the name of a dervish Order.

**MEVLĀNA** Arabic word meaning 'our master'; most commonly, but not exclusively, used of Jelāl ed-Din Rūmi. (*See* Introduction.)

**MIR'ĀJ** Means 'ascension' in Arabic. Used in reference to the event described in Sura (Chapter) 17.1 of the Koran: 'Celebrated be the praises of Him who took His servant a journey by night from the Sacred Mosque [at Mecca] to the Remote Mosque [at Jerusalem] . . . 'The Night of the Ascent is a most sacred night celebrated by devout Moslems in prayer.

**MIHRĀB** *See* KIBLĒ above.

**MUEZZIN** He who makes the Call to Prayer (Ezan), most usually from the minaret of a mosque, for each of the five daily prayers. The Ezan for the early morning prayer includes the sentence, repeated: 'Prayer is better than sleep.'

**MUFTI** One learned in Moslem jurisprudence holding an office requiring him to interpret the Canon Law on all cases submitted to him.

**MUNKĪR (and NEKĪR)** The two angels who will question each soul on the Day of Judgement.

**MURSHĪD** A spiritual mentor and guide to a *murīd* (his follower or postulant).

**MUSTAFA** An honorific, meaning the 'chosen one', of the Prophet Mohammed.

**NEKĪR** *See* MUNKĪR above.
**NŪSHIRVĀN** *See* FERIDŪN above.

**OMAR-i HATTĀB** The second Successor (Caliph) to the Prophet Mohammed.

**ar-RAHMĀN** One of the many Attributes, or Names of God. Its meaning is 'the Merciful'. Is included in the sentence of recollection at the beginning of each Sura (Chapter) of the Koran, save one, and used before starting any undertaking: 'In the name of God, the Merciful, the Compassionate' (*Bismī'llahi 'rrahmāni 'rrahīm*).
**RIDVĀN** The angel holding the keys to Paradise.
**RŪM** Rome, hence the (Eastern) Roman Empire. Later used to signify the European lands of the Ottoman Empire; the lands west of the Bosphorus being Rumeli, and on the east Anadolu (Anatolia).

**SELMĀN** A Persian Moslem convert contemporary with the Prophet Mohammed.
**SALTŪK** The predecessor of BARĀK *see* above.
**ash-SHÂM** Damascus, signifying northern Arabia, especially Syria.
**SHERĪK** Means 'partner'. The formula *Lā sherīk* ('There is no partner' – with God, to be understood) is a Moslem affirmation of the absolute unity of the Godhead. It is quoted in Yunus's Verse 89.
**SHERI'ĀT** The Moslem corpus of jurisprudence, derived from the Koran itself and the Holy Traditions of the Prophet Mohammed, which together constitute the two sources of orthodoxy.
**as-SIRĀT** The bridge, finer than a hair, sharper than a sword, by which each must cross after death.
**SHIRĪN** *See* FERHĀD above.
**SHEYKH** Elder, old man. Normally a term of respect accorded to the head of an Arab tribe; but derivatively the title of the head of a dervish Order or of an individual dervish convent.
**SOLOMON** Was conceived as holding sway over the spirits (jinns) lower than angels, and the world of fairies (peris). The reference in Yunus's Verse 37 is to Sura (Chapter) 27.17–18 of the Koran:

> And assembled for Solomon were his hosts ... Said an ant, 'O ye ants! Go into your dwellings that Solomon and his hosts crush you not unwittingly.' And he smiled in amusement at her speech, and said, 'O Lord! Stir me to be thankful for Thy favour, which Thou hast bestowed on me and my parents, and to do righteousness which shall please Thee; and make me enter into Thy mercy among Thy righteous servants.'

The reference in Verse 48 is to Sura 27.16: 'And Solomon ... said, "O ye folk! We have been taught the speech of birds" ...' The phrase 'speech of birds' (*mantiq at-tayyir*) is the title of an allegorical poem by Farid ed-Din Attar (died 1221) which is usually translated in English as *The Conference of the Birds*. The poem relates how the birds set out in search of their mysterious king, the Simurgh. (Their leader is the Hoopoe mentioned in the same Sura 27 as conveying messages between Solomon and the Queen of Sheba.) The following condensation of Attar's poem is also taken from the Oxford University Press publication referred to above under MANSŪR al-HALLĀJ:

> After traversing the seven valleys of Search, Love, Knowledge, Detachment, Unity, Bewilderment, and Self-noughting, the survivors, thirty in number, are admitted to his presence and realize that 'they themselves are the Simurgh, while the Simurgh is nothing but those thirty birds (*si murgh*).'

**TAPTŪK**   Taptūk Baba (Father Taptūk) was Yunus Emre's *Murshīd*, q.v. above. The word *taptūk* in Turkish means 'we have found' or 'we have met'. (Some commentators have seen Yunus's use of the word to signify the Godhead.)

**TĀRIKAT**   Turkish form of an Arabic word (*tāriqa*) meaning a 'way', or 'path'; used to denote the various dervish Orders or Brotherhoods.

**VEZIR**   The Counsellor or Minister of a ruler.

**ZULEIKA**   The name of Potiphar's wife.

**ZUNNĀR**   Rope girdle worn by Christians (especially monks and friars) but used to signify any kind of imperfect belief – or, very rarely, dedication.

# INDEX OF TURKISH
# INITIAL LINES

Where the translation has taken a couplet as a whole both lines are given.

1  Bir şâha kul olmak gerek hergiz ma'zûl olmaz ola
2  Aceb aceb ne nesnedir bu derd ile firâk bana
3  Gider idim ben yol sıra yavlak uzamış bir ağaç
4  Sen bu cihan mülkünü kaftan-kafa tuttun tut
5  Işk imamdır bize gönül cemâat
6  Din ü millet sorarısan âşıklara din ne hâcet
7  Sabahın sinliye vardım gördüm cümle ölmüş yatur
8  Yeryüzünde gezer idim uğradım milketler yatur
9  Bu dünyanın meseli bir ulu şara benzer
10 İlim ilim bilmektir ilim kendin bilmektir
11 Bu dem yüzüm süre-duram her dem Ayım yeni doğar
12 Nite ki bu gönlüm evi ışk elinden taşa-gelir
13 Hak bir gönül verdi bana hâ demeden hayrân olur
14 İşidin ey yârenler ışk bir güneşe benzer
15 Tanrı'yiçin canım canı cefâyise tapdur yeter
16 Benim gönlüm-gözüm ışktan doludur
    Dilim söyle yâri yüzüm suludur
17 Ne bilsin bu aşkı usanlar uyalar
18 Erenler nazarında sofuluk satmayalar
19 Yar yüreğim yar gör ki neler var
20 Dost senin ışkın oku key katı candan geçer
21 Hakıykat erenleri şer'ile bilmediler
22 Bilirmişiz ey yârenler gerçek erenler kandadır
23 Söylemek harcısı söylemeğin hasıdır
24 Evliyâya münkirler Hak yoluna âsıdır
25 Ey dost seni severim can içre yerin vardır
26 Ey dost senin ışkın odu ciğerim pâre-baş kılur
27 İşbu vücud şehrine her dem giresim gelir
28 Ey bana iyi diyen benim kamudan kemter

131

29  Keleci bilen kişinin yüzünü ağ ede bir söz
30  Hiç bir kimse bilmez bizi biz ne işin içindeyiz
31  Nidem ben bu gönül ile benim ile bile durmaz
32  Yârab bu ne derttir derman bulunmaz
33  Bize didâr gerek dünya gerekmez
34  Ben dervişim diyen kişi işbu yola âr gerekmez
      Derviş olan kişilerin gönlü ginğdir dar gerekmez
35  Gayrıdır her milletten bu bizim milletimiz
36  Sûfiyim halk içinde tesbih elimden gitmez
37  Erenlerin yolları inceden inceymiş
38  Kerem et bir beri bak nikâbı yüzünden bırak
39  Ey çok kitaplar okuyan çünkim tutarsın bana dak
40  Biz kime âşıksavuz âlemler ona âşık
41  Mâ'ni evine daldık vücud seyrini kıldık
42  Ne söz keleci derisem dilim seni söyleyecek
43  Nideriz hayat suyun biz can yağmaya verdik
44  Eya gönül açgıl gözün fikrin yavlak uzatmagıl
45  Işksızlara verme öğüt öğüdünden alır değil
46  Canlar fedâ yoluna bu can kaygısı değil
47  Mâ'ni eri bu yolda melûl olası değil
48  Senin ben demekliğin mâ'nide usûl değil
49  Tehi görme kimseyi hiç kimsene boş değil
50  Bir kez gönül yıktınısa bu kıldığın namaz değil
51  Kul pâdşahsız olmaz pâdişah kulsuz değil
52  Dervişlik dedikleri hırka ile taç değil
53  Bir nazarda kalmayalım gel dosta gidelim gönül
54  Ata belinden bir zaman anasına düştü gönül
55  Hiç bilmezem kezek kimin aramızda gezer ölüm
56  Teferrüc eyleyivardım sabahın sinleri gördüm
57  Sensin Kerîm Sensin Rahîm Allah sana sundum elim
58  Bu mülke garip geldim ben bu elden bezerim
59  Dosttan haber geldi bana duralım andan varayım
60  Benim bunda kararım yok ben bundan gitmeğe geldim
61  Beni bunda veribiyen bilir ben ne işe geldim
62  Her nereye döner isem ışk iledir işim benim
63  Tehî görmen siz beni dost yüzün görüp geldim
64  Dost bakalı yüzüme ben şehi görüp geldim
65  Ey yârenler ey kardeşler sorun bana kandayıdım
66  Aldı benim gönlümü nolduğunu bilmezem
67  Uş gene geldim ki bunda sır sözün iyân eyleyim

68   Kâ'be vü büt iman benim çark uruban dönen benim
69   Muhammed ile bile mi'râca ağan benim
70   Ben bende buldum çün Hak'ı şekk ü güman nemdir benim
71   Evvel benim âhır benim canlara can olan benim
72   Benim ol tılsım-ı pinhân ki bugün iyâna geldim
73   Ne der isem yortum yürür elimde ferman tutarım
74   Ey dost ışkın denizine girem gark olam yürüyem
75   Hak Çalabım Hak Çalabım sencileyin yok Çalabım
76   Bu fenâ mülkünde ben nice nice hayrân olam
77   Nitekim ben beni bildim yakın bil ki Hakk'ı buldum
78   Deniz oldu bir kaç kadeh susalığım kanmaz benim
79   Ey bana derviş diyen nem ola derviş benim
80   Aceb şu yerde var m'ola şöyle garib bencileyin
81   Gönül usandın sen bu seferden
82   Kanda bulayım isteyüben ey gönül seni kandasın
     Kanda virâne varısa vallâhi gönül andasın
83   Taştın yine deli gönül sular gibi çağlar mısın
84   Ol dost bize gelmez ise ben dosta girü varayın
85   Şöyle hayrân eyle beni ışkın oduna yanayın
86   Ol dürr-i yetimem ki görmedi beni ummân
87   Din ü millet kodurdu ol benim canım alan
88   Bugün sohbet bizim oldu bize bizim diyen gelsin
89   Lâ şerik'ten okursun yine şerik katarsın
90   Aşıkız ne diyelim ışk haberinden şirin
91   Canlar canını buldum bu canım yağma olsun
92   Gözüm seni görmek için elim sana ermek için
93   Çalap nûrdan yaratmış canını Muhammed'in
94   Işk eri haberini aydam işide misin
95   Zinhâr vermegil gönül dünya pâyına bir gün
96   Dervişlerin yoluna sıdk ile gelen gelsin
97   Ey bana iyi diyen adımı sûfi koyan
98   Sana derim ey veli dur erte namazına
99   Bu dünyanın misâli benzer bir değirmene
100  Gene bu bâd-ı nevbahar hoş nev'ile esti gene
101  Her kime kim dervişlik bağışlana
102  İki cihan zindan ise gerek bana bostan ola
103  Bir kez yüzünü gören ömrünce unutmaya
104  Hak'tan inen şerbeti içtik el hamdü lillah
105  Dirliğim neyidiğin aydayım kıldan kıla
106  Ey kopuz ile çeşte aslın nedürür işte

107   İstediğimi buldum eşkere can içinde
108   Ey ışk delisi olan ne kaldın perâkende
109   Bir Ay gördüm bu gece kamu burclardan yüce
110   Âşık oldum erene ermek ile
111   Mâ'ni beratın aldık uş gene elimize
112   Miskinlik ile gelsin kimde erlik varısa
113   Bir söz diyeyim sana dinle canın varısa
114   Hakk'ı kaçan bulasın Hakk'a kul olmayınca
115   Aklım başıma gelmedi ışk şarâbın tatmayınca
116   Sensiz yola girerisem çârem yok adım atmağa
117   Bî mekânım bu cihanda menzil ü durağım onda
118   Sana ibret gerek ise gel göresin bu sinleri
119   Yok yere geçirdim günü ah nideyim ömrüm seni
120   Geldi geçti ömrüm benim şol yel esip geçmiş gibi
121   Düşd'önüme hubbül vatan gidem hey dost deyi deyi
122   Banladı ol müezzin durdu kaamet eyledi
123   Ben yürürüm yana yana aşk boyadı beni kana
124   Işk ile isteridik gene bulduk ol canı
125   Işk bezirgânı sermâye canı
126   Evvel dahı varıdı canımda bu ışk odu
127   Yine yüzünü gördüm yine yüreğim yandı
128   Kaçan ol mahbûb-i cihan benim gözüme tuş oldu
129   Yort ey gönül sen bir zaman âsûde fariğ koş yürü
130   Uş yine ışkın beni mest ü harâb eyledi
131   Ben bunda seyeder iken aceb sırra erdim ahi
132   Erenler bir denizdir âşık gerek dalası
        Bahrı gerek denizden girip cevher alası
133   Bencileyin gören kişi ben sevdiğimin yüzünü
134   Ol Çalab'ımın ışkı bağrımı baş eyledi
135   Doldur kadeh sungıl bize ışk şarabından ey sâki
136   Bu ışk denizine dalan hâcet değil ona gemi
137   Hak nûru âşıklara her dem nüzûl değil mi
138   Işkın aldı benden beni bana seni gerek seni
139   Bir sâkiden içtik şarâb Arş'tan yüce meyhânesi
140   Dilsizler haberini kulaksız dinleyesi
141   Nice bir besleyesin bu kadd ile kaameti
142   Helâl kıldı ma'şûka âşık kendi kanını
143   Evvel dost bizden yana bilmeyiz nice baktı
144   Ey yârenler aydımazam canım neye daldığını
145   Bir suâlim var sana ey dervişler ecesi

146   Benim zâri kılan şol yâre karşı
147   Erenlerin gönlünde ol sultan dükân açtı
148   Baktığım yüzde gördüm Taptuk'umun nârunu
149   Dinin imanın varısa hor görmegil dervişleri
150   İşidin ey yârenler eve dervişler geldi
151   Beni melâmet eyledi bu ne aceb sevdâyıdı
152   Çıktım erik dalına anda yedim üzümü
153   Bana namaz kılmaz diyen ben kılarım namazımı
154   Ey yârenler kim işitti âşık tövbe kıldığını
155   Severem ben seni candan içeri
156   İster idim Allah'ı buldumsa ne oldu
157   Yâ ilâhi ger suâl etsen bana